AF429268

WHOSE SHOES ARE THESE?

WHOSE SHOES ARE THESE?

by

Holly Hunter Harris

Bell Street Publishing

Cover Design: Rodney Harris, Sr.

Whose Shoes Are These?

This book is a work of nonfiction. The views expressed are those of the author, based on research, experience, and reflection. Any references to events, individuals, or organizations are intended to support the narrative and arc not meant to defame, infringe on rights, or misrepresent any person or group.

First Edition

Bell Street Publishing

Table of Contents

Foreword

In a world where family dynamics constantly evolve, children's emotional and psychological well-being in single-parent households is often overlooked. One significant factor is the frequent introduction of new romantic partners into the single-parent family setting and home, which can profoundly affect a child's sense of stability and security.

This book, 'Whose Shoes Are These?', explores the far-reaching consequences of such instability on children's development, relationships, and emotional health. Careful analysis and practical strategies offer single parents a roadmap for balancing their personal lives while prioritizing their children's emotional well-being.

"Whose Shoes" aims to help parents foster a stable environment where their children can thrive by providing insights into the impact of frequent partner introductions. Addressing the delicate balance between dating and parenting, it emphasizes the need for clear boundaries, open communication, and consistent routines, ultimately guiding single parents toward creating a loving, secure family dynamic.

Let this book serve as a compassionate resource for parents navigating the complexities of modern relationships, offering thoughtful advice to ensure that children remain emotionally secure throughout the change process.

Chapter 1

Understanding the Impact of Instability

In today's society, single-parent families face numerous challenges, one of the most significant being the frequent introduction of new romantic partners into the home. While dating and forming new relationships are natural aspects of life, the instability these relationships create for children can have profound emotional and psychological consequences, especially when partners are introduced without a long-term commitment.

The Shifting Landscape of Family Dynamics
The erosion of traditional family structures can be traced to various factors, including shifting societal norms, economic pressures, and increased divorce rates. As work demands grew and families became more disconnected, emotional bonds within the household weakened. Over time, the family unit, once anchored by close relationships and traditions, fragmented, leading to an increase in single-parent homes. In earlier generations, elders often played a crucial role in providing stability and support within the family. Still, in today's world, grandparents may

live far away, be deceased, or not have strong bonds with their children or grandchildren.

The rise of cohabitation without marriage has become a prominent feature of modern relationships, driven by changing values prioritizing personal freedoms and financial independence. More parents are raising children outside of marriage, often without long-term commitments between partners. This shift has contributed to instability for children who grow up in environments where healthy relationships are short-lived, transient, or non-existent.

In addition to these societal changes, the increased acceptance of blended families has added another layer of complexity to modern family dynamics. While blended families can be rich and rewarding, they also require careful navigation to ensure children feel secure and valued. For children, frequent changes in family composition—such as new step-siblings, step-parents, or other transient figures—can create a sense of instability, leading them to question where they fit in the family structure.

Economic Pressures and the Breakdown of Commitment

In the past, marriage was seen as a lifelong commitment, often entered with a strong sense of purpose and duty. However, many modern relationships begin optimistically but become strained over time due to work pressures, financial instability, and emotional disconnection. Economic challenges play a significant role in shaping these dynamics. As financial strains increase, so does the likelihood of conflict, stress, and emotional disengagement between partners. External distractions and infidelity further erode trust and commitment, leaving many marriages unable to withstand the pressures of modern life. For either partner, it is perceived to be easier for them to dissolve the relationship and go their separate ways. Rarely are the children's emotions, development, or welfare, as a whole, considered.

Single parents' economic pressures often compound the difficulties of dating and forming new relationships. Financial instability can lead to an increased dependence on romantic partners, sometimes resulting in rushed or poorly considered introductions of new partners to children. When parents struggle to make ends meet, they may see a new partner as a potential source of financial support, which can blur the lines between practical necessity and emotional readiness.

As divorce rates skyrocketed in the late twentieth century, more and more children found themselves in single-parent homes, often dealing with the fallout of their parents' dissolved commitments. For these children, the emotional and psychological toll can be immense, leaving them with a distorted view of relationships, trust, and security. The instability created by frequent changes in their primary caregiver's romantic life can lead children to internalize feelings of inadequacy, believing they are at fault for the instability they experience.

Emotional Consequences for Children
Children are particularly vulnerable to the effects of frequent partner introductions, as they rely on their parents for emotional stability and security. When new romantic partners enter and exit their lives without permanence, children often struggle to form lasting attachments and may develop a deep sense of emotional insecurity. This lack of stability can lead to feelings of abandonment, confusion, and mistrust.

Children in these environments may experience a range of emotional and behavioral issues, such as:

Anxiety and Clinginess: Younger children may become anxious or overly dependent on their parents, fearing that they may also lose their parents' attention. This anxiety often manifests in clingy behavior, where the child needs to remain physically close to the parent to ensure they are not forgotten.

Rebellion and Defiance: Adolescents may act out or become defiant, struggling to process their emotions or feeling powerless to control the changes happening in their homes. This rebellion is often an expression of frustration and a way to regain some control over their lives. They may push boundaries and test limits, seeking reassurance that, despite changes, they are still valued and loved.

Mistrust of Relationships: Over time, these children may internalize the instability they've experienced, leading to difficulties in forming healthy relationships later in life. The belief that relationships are temporary and unreliable can become deeply ingrained, making it challenging for them to trust others or invest emotionally in long-term commitments.

Children may also struggle with an identity crisis as they try to understand their place within a constantly changing family structure. When new partners come and go, children may begin to question whether they are worthy of stable, lasting love. This lack of a stable foundation can lead to low self-esteem, a fear of abandonment, and a reluctance to form attachments, both in childhood and later in adult relationships.

The Role of Grandparents and Extended Family
Historically, grandparents played a crucial role in supporting and nurturing their grandchildren. They provided wisdom, stability, and a connection to family traditions. Today, however, that dynamic has shifted. Many grandparents live far from their grandchildren or cannot maintain close relationships due to family conflicts, unresolved issues with their children, or simply being too far removed, age-

related, from the family's day-to-day life. When grandparents take on the responsibility of raising their grandchildren, they offer the benefit of seasoned parenting experience, often stepping in when the child's parent is unable or unwilling to fulfill their role. However, relying on grandparents to raise children can be a strain, mainly if the grandparents are not financially or physically equipped to handle the child's demands. Nevertheless, their involvement can provide a much-needed sense of stability for children who otherwise experience frequent disruptions in their home lives.

Grandparents can serve as a stabilizing force, offering a sense of continuity in the face of change. They can provide children with an unchanging source of love and support, particularly important when other aspects of their lives feel uncertain. However, the effectiveness of this support often depends on the strength of the grandparent-grandchild relationship and the level of involvement the grandparents can maintain. In situations where grandparents are present and actively engaged, children may better cope with the instability created by frequent partner introductions.

The Importance of Routine and Predictability
Children thrive on routine and predictability, which provides them with a sense of security and helps them feel in control of their environment. Introducing new partners into the household often disrupts

established routines, leading to confusion and emotional upheaval for children. The sudden presence of a new adult in their home can alter everything from bedtime rituals to family mealtimes, which can be unsettling for children who rely on these routines for comfort and stability. Maintaining consistency in daily routines, regardless of the presence of a new partner, is crucial for minimizing the negative impact on children. Parents should strive to keep critical aspects of their child's day-to-day life consistent— such as meal times, bedtimes, and school routines—even when navigating new relationships. This predictability helps children feel secure and reassures them that the core elements of their lives remain stable despite changes in the family dynamic.

Parents should also communicate openly with their children about changes that may occur when introducing a new partner. Preparing children in advance, answering their questions honestly, and involving them in discussions about how their routines might be affected can help alleviate uncertainty and fear. Children must understand that while some things may change, their needs will always be prioritized.

The Emotional Toll of Parental Inattention
Another significant consequence of frequent partner introductions is the potential for parental inattention. Parents focused on building new romantic

relationships may unintentionally neglect their child's emotional needs. Children may feel they are no longer a priority, leading to feelings of abandonment and low self-worth. This perception is particularly harmful when a new partner receives more attention than the child, reinforcing the idea that the child is less important. Parental inattention can also exacerbate behavioral problems. Children may act out in an attempt to regain their parent's attention, even if the attention they receive is negative. They may engage in disruptive behaviors, struggle academically, or withdraw socially as they attempt to process the emotional impact of feeling sidelined. Parents must be mindful of the potential for their new relationship to inadvertently take precedence over their child's needs and make a concerted effort to provide emotional support and reassurance.

Spending dedicated one-on-one time with the child is essential in mitigating these effects. Simple activities like reading together, playing games, or just talking about their day can help children feel valued and secure. Parents can help counteract the adverse effects of perceived inattention by ensuring their child feels seen and heard.

Case Study 1: Jamie's Struggle with Relationship Instability

Jamie, a 9-year-old boy, faced significant challenges when his single mother began dating again. Each new partner was introduced into Jamie's life with little preparation, causing confusion and emotional distress. As these adults came and went, Jamie struggled to understand why they appeared, only to leave shortly after that. This inconsistency made Jamie feel insecure and unsure about who he could rely on, leading him to withdraw from his family and social circles.

The impact of these changes became evident in Jamie's behavior at school. He experienced frequent emotional outbursts, often triggered by seemingly minor issues. His grades also began to decline, as he found it challenging to concentrate amidst the emotional turmoil at home. Jamie's teachers reported that he seemed distracted, anxious, and increasingly reluctant to participate in class activities. The instability in his home life was taking a toll on his overall well-being.

At home, Jamie's withdrawal became more pronounced. He became less interested in activities he once enjoyed, such as playing soccer and spending time with friends. Instead, he spent more time alone, retreating to his room after school. Initially unaware of Jamie's distress, his mother assumed he needed time to adjust. However, as Jamie's behavior continued to deteriorate, she realized the impact her dating life was having on her son.

Recognizing the need for intervention, Jamie's mother sought professional help. Together, they began working with a therapist who specialized in family dynamics and childhood anxiety. Through therapy, Jamie's mother learned about the importance of providing her son with stability and predictability, especially during periods of change. The therapist emphasized that Jamie needed to feel secure in his environment and that sudden introductions of new partners disrupted his sense of safety.

The therapist also worked directly with Jamie, helping him articulate his feelings about the changes in his family. Jamie said he often felt "forgotten" or "pushed aside" whenever a new partner entered their lives. He feared that his mother's attention would be permanently diverted, leaving him without the emotional support he needed. These fears fueled his anxiety and led to the behaviors he exhibited both at home and in school. Through consistent sessions, Jamie and his mother developed strategies to cope with these challenges. Jamie's mother learned to gradually introduce new people into their lives, ensuring Jamie had time to adjust before a new partner became a significant presence. She also concerted effort to reassure Jamie that he would always be her top priority regardless of new relationships. By dedicating regular one-on-one time to Jamie—whether through shared activities or simply talking- she helped rebuild his trust and sense of security.

Jamie, in turn, learned coping techniques to manage his anxiety. The therapist introduced him to mindfulness exercises, such as deep breathing and guided imagery, which helped him stay calm during moments of stress. Jamie also benefited from having a safe space to express his fears and concerns openly, without fear of judgment. This open communication helped him feel more in control and less overwhelmed by the changes around him.

Over time, Jamie's anxiety began to reduce. He started to re-engage with his schoolwork, and his grades improved. His emotional outbursts became less frequent, and he began participating in class activities again. Jamie grew more comfortable at home, and his relationship with his mother strengthened. He felt reassured by her commitment to providing a stable environment and appreciated the gradual approach to introducing new people into their lives.

This case study highlights the importance of considering a child's emotional needs when navigating changes in family dynamics. Stability and predictability are critical components of a child's emotional well-being. Sudden changes, such as frequent introductions of new partners, can create feelings of insecurity and anxiety. By recognizing these challenges and seeking professional guidance, Jamie's mother made a more nurturing and stable environment, ultimately helping her son regain his confidence and emotional balance.

Parents in similar situations can learn from Jamie's experience. Introducing new relationships should be done carefully, considering the child's needs and ensuring they feel included and valued. Consistent communication, reassurance, and familiar routines can significantly reduce the negative impacts of family changes, allowing children to thrive amidst evolving dynamics.

Conclusion: Prioritizing Children's Emotional Well-Being

The root of this issue is the breakdown of stable family structures. While changing societal norms have shifted how families are formed and maintained, children's emotional and psychological needs remain constant. Children require stability, consistency, and emotional support to thrive, and when these elements are absent, the consequences can be profound and long-lasting.

This book will continue to explore how frequent partner introductions affect children's development and offer guidance for single parents seeking to balance their emotional needs with their children's well-being. By fostering an environment of stability, open communication, and consistent support, parents can help their children navigate the complexities of modern family life and emerge with the resilience and emotional health necessary to build fulfilling relationships in the future.

By better understanding these dynamics, parents can make more informed decisions about how they approach relationships and create an environment that prioritizes their children's emotional health and security. By putting their children's well-being first and being mindful of how new relationships affect the family dynamic, parents can help mitigate the negative impacts of instability and foster a nurturing, supportive home where children feel safe, valued, and loved.

Chapter 2

Short-Term Emotional Instability

Frequent partner introductions into the home can cause immediate emotional instability in children as they struggle to understand the new adult's role in their lives. Depending on the child's age and developmental stage, this confusion and insecurity can manifest in various ways. Addressing these emotional challenges requires empathy, consistency, and an understanding of the underlying fears driving a child's behaviors.

Effects on Younger Children
Young children, in particular, are highly susceptible to emotional distress when faced with frequent changes in their home environment. At this developmental stage, children rely heavily on routine, consistency, and stable attachments to feel secure. The introduction of new partners disrupts their sense of normalcy, often leading to behaviors that signal distress:

Clinginess and Separation Anxiety: Younger children may become excessively clingy, refusing to leave their parent's side or showing anxiety when separated. This behavior stems from the child's need for reassurance in the face of perceived instability. Their world, which should feel safe and predictable, is shaken by the presence of unfamiliar adults who come and go. To mitigate this, parents can create routines that remain unchanged regardless of a new partner's presence. Reassurance through words and actions, such as spending dedicated time with the child, can also help reduce anxiety.

Regressive Behaviors: Children may regress in certain areas, such as bedwetting, thumb-sucking, or reverting to baby talk, as their way to cope with emotional insecurity. These regressive behaviors reflect the child's attempt to return to an earlier stage of life when they felt more secure and protected. It is crucial to provide comfort without judgment in these moments. Parents should avoid scolding the child for regressive behaviors and instead offer extra affection and patience, reinforcing a sense of safety and security.

Crying and Emotional Outbursts: Young children may also exhibit unexplained crying or emotional outbursts as they struggle to process the changes around them. They often lack the verbal skills to articulate their feelings, so they express them through tears or tantrums.

Parents must acknowledge their children's emotions, even if they seem irrational. Offering comfort and helping the child name their feelings—such as saying, "I can see that you're feeling sad or scared"—can help children feel understood and gradually develop better emotional regulation skills.

Feelings of Abandonment: When a new partner takes up a significant amount of the parent's time and attention, the child may feel abandoned or neglected. Young children often equate love with time spent together, and any perceived reduction in parental attention can leave them feeling forgotten. Parents should make a concerted effort to spend time with their children one-on-one, ensuring their bond remains strong. Small gestures, like bedtime stories or shared activities, can reassure children that they remain a priority.

Effects on Adolescents

For adolescents, the emotional consequences of frequent partner introductions often manifest in more complex and severe ways. Adolescents are at a critical stage of developing their identity and independence, and disruptions in their home life can cause feelings of anger, confusion, and mistrust:

Rebellion and Defiance: Adolescents may act out by rebelling against their parents' authority or deliberately defying household rules. This behavior is often a way for teens to exert control when they feel powerless. As new partners enter the home, adolescent children may resist any attempts by these individuals to establish authority or influence household dynamics. Parents should avoid forcing relationships between their children and new partners. Allowing their children to set boundaries and express their feelings can help them feel respected and reduce defiant behaviors. Instead of demanding compliance, parents can facilitate open conversations that encourage understanding and compromise.

Disrespect Toward Authority: Teenagers who witness a revolving door of new partners may lose respect for the latest adults and their parents. The constant changes can lead them to question their parents' judgment and decision-making, resulting in a strained relationship between parent and child. This disrespect may extend beyond the home, affecting their interactions with teachers, coaches, and other authority figures. Parents should demonstrate consistency in their actions and decisions to rebuild respect. Teens are more likely to respect parents who show thoughtfulness and care when making choices that affect the family. Apologizing for mistakes and acknowledging the teen's perspective can also go a long way in repairing strained relationships.

Aggression and Behavioral Issues: In some cases, emotional instability can lead to aggression, either toward the parent, new partner, or even peers and siblings. Teens struggling to cope with the instability in their home lives may channel their frustration through violence or disruptive behaviors at school. Addressing these behaviors requires identifying their root cause, often the fear of being replaced or forgotten. Parents should provide emotional support, offer outlets for stress, such as physical activities or creative hobbies, and consider seeking professional help if aggressive behavior persists.

Social Withdrawal: Adolescents may also withdraw from social interactions, feeling embarrassed or ashamed of their home life. This withdrawal can lead to isolation, as teens avoid discussing their family situation with friends or peers, further deepening their emotional struggles. Encouraging teens to maintain friendships and participate in extracurricular activities can help mitigate social withdrawal. Providing a safe space at home to talk about their feelings without fear of judgment is also crucial for helping them navigate their emotions.

Loss of Trust and Security
Trust is a foundational element of a child's emotional stability, and frequent changes in the home can significantly erode that trust. Regardless of age, children rely on their parents to provide a safe, secure environment. When the constant introduction of new partners compromises this stability, the child's trust in their parents—and authority figures more broadly—begins to break down.

Mistrust of Authority: Children may lose faith in their parents' ability to provide a secure and stable home. This mistrust can extend to other authority figures in their life, such as teachers, relatives, or even future romantic partners. The inability to rely on adults to remain consistent and dependable can make it difficult for children to form stable bonds as they grow older. Rebuilding trust takes time and requires consistency. Parents should prioritize transparency, explain changes in advance, and involve children in age-appropriate discussions. This approach helps demonstrate that, while some things may change, the parent's commitment to the child's well-being remains unwavering.

Emotional Detachment: Some children may emotionally distance themselves from new partners or even their parents as a coping mechanism. This emotional distance protects them from the potential harm of forming attachments that would likely be disrupted. While this detachment may provide temporary relief, it can hinder the child's emotional development and ability to create meaningful relationships in the future.

Case Study 2: Mia's Journey Through Relationship Instability

Mia, a 14-year-old girl, faced emotional challenges as her mother's romantic relationships changed every few months. Each new partner was introduced into Mia's life without much warning, which left her feeling neglected and unsure of her place in her mother's priorities. The lack of stability at home took a toll on Mia's emotional well-being, and her resentment began manifesting in her behavior. Mia's grades started slipping, and she began skipping school and avoiding her friends. She distanced herself from her family, retreating into her world as a way of coping with the constant changes around her.

Mia rebelled to express her frustration and cries for help. She felt disconnected from her mother, who seemed more focused on her relationships than her needs. The lack of consistent attention left Mia feeling like she was always second-best, making it difficult to trust her mother and other adults. The frequent introductions of new partners led Mia to believe that relationships were fleeting and unreliable, which impacted her ability to form meaningful connections with others.

Mia's mother eventually realized that her approach to dating was negatively affecting her daughter. Seeing her daughter's declining school performance, withdrawal from family activities, and increasingly defiant behavior was a wake-up call. Mia's mother decided to step back and reevaluate how her choices impacted her daughter. She understood that her daughter needed stability and reassurance and to feel that she was a priority, especially during such a formative period in her life.

Determined to rebuild her relationship with Mia, her mother initiated a series of open and honest conversations. She sat down with Mia and gave her space to express her feelings, which had not happened before. Mia was initially hesitant, but she began to open up with time. She expressed her anger and sadness over feeling replaced whenever a new partner entered their lives. Mia's mother listened attentively without dismissing her feelings or trying to defend her actions. This act of listening was a crucial turning point—it showed Mia that her mother genuinely cared about her feelings and was willing to change.

From then on, Mia's mother adopted a more thoughtful approach regarding her romantic life. Instead of introducing new partners immediately, she waited until the relationship was serious and stable. She also involved Mia in the process, letting her know beforehand and asking her thoughts. This helped Mia feel more included and less blindsided by sudden changes. Her mother also made a conscious effort to spend quality one-on-one time with Mia, ensuring their bond remained strong and that Mia knew she was valued above all else.

Mia's mother also sought the help of a family therapist to facilitate their communication and help them navigate their complex emotions. The therapist provided Mia and her mother with tools to better understand each other's perspectives. Mia learned coping mechanisms to manage her feelings of jealousy and fear of abandonment, while her mother learned how to balance her personal needs with her responsibilities as a parent. The therapy sessions provided a safe space for both to express their concerns and work towards rebuilding their trust.

Over time, these changes began to have a positive impact. Mia's behavior gradually improved—she started attending school regularly again, and her grades began to recover. She also became more engaged in family activities and increased her interest in reconnecting with her friends. The resentment she had felt towards her mother began to dissipate as she saw that her mother was making a genuine effort to prioritize her well-being. Mia's trust in her mother slowly returned, and with it, her confidence in the stability of her home life.

This case study highlights the importance of prioritizing a child's emotional needs when navigating new relationships. For teenagers like Mia, the stability of their home environment is crucial to their emotional and psychological development. By listening to Mia and involving her in decisions that affected their family, her mother was able to repair their relationship and provide Mia with the security she needed. The shift from neglecting Mia's emotional needs to actively prioritizing them was transformative, helping Mia regain her trust and belonging.

Parents in similar situations can learn valuable lessons from Mia's experience. Introducing new partners should be done thoughtfully and with the child's feelings in mind. Open communication, reassurance, and consistency are critical factors in ensuring children feel secure and valued, even as family dynamics evolve. Parents can create a supportive environment where their children can thrive by making them feel like an integral part of the family and taking their emotional needs seriously.

Parents should strive to create an environment where emotional expression is encouraged and validated. By consistently showing empathy and interest in the child's feelings, parents can gradually break down the barriers children build to protect themselves from emotional pain.

Behavioral Reactions to Compete for Attention
In situations where a parent's attention shifts more towards a new partner, children may engage in behaviors aimed at competing for their parent's affection and time. This is a natural behavior and must be positively acknowledged by the parent and the new partner.

Misinformation and Deception: Children may mislead their new partner or parent, intentionally creating misunderstandings to drive a wedge between them. This behavior is often motivated by jealousy or fear of losing their parents' attention. Parents should consider this behavior a cry for help rather than a form of manipulation. Open, honest conversations with the child about their feelings and reassurance of their importance in the parent's life can help reduce the need for such behaviors.

Destructive Behavior: Children may resort to theft, destruction of personal belongings, or creating tension by bringing up the other parent or past partners to destabilize the new relationship. These actions are often fueled by a desire to regain control over a situation threatening their emotional security. Addressing these behaviors involves recognizing the underlying emotions driving them—fear, anger, or sadness. Providing consistent love, setting clear and firm boundaries, and reinforcing positive behaviors can help guide children toward healthier ways of expressing their emotions.

Testing Boundaries: Children may intentionally test to gain more attention or see how far they can push the new partner or their parent. This behavior reflects the child's need for reassurance and emotional validation in a time of uncertainty.

Parents should respond to boundary testing with patience and consistency. It's crucial to reinforce boundaries while also acknowledging the child's feelings. This approach helps children understand that boundaries are in place to ensure their safety and well-being, not as punishment.

Conclusion: Addressing Short-Term Emotional Instability

Short-term emotional instability is a natural response for children facing frequent changes in their home environments. By recognizing these behaviors as signals of more profound emotional distress, parents can take proactive steps to mitigate the negative impacts on their children. Open communication, consistent boundaries, and prioritizing the child's emotional needs can help create a more stable environment, even as family dynamics evolve.

Parents should also consider seeking professional support when needed. Therapists or counselors can offer valuable guidance, help children healthily process their emotions, and equip parents with strategies to foster a supportive and stable home environment. Ultimately, understanding and addressing short-term emotional instability is about creating a foundation of trust, empathy, and security, allowing children to thrive even amid changes.

Chapter 3

Long-Term Psychological Health

The long-term psychological effects of frequent partner introductions in a child's life are profoundly concerning and can manifest far beyond childhood. While the immediate impacts are often visible in behaviors and emotional outbursts, the more profound, lasting effects shape a child's mental health, self-image, and ability to form relationships as they mature. These experiences can cause children to develop a distorted perception of relationships, and they often struggle to create healthy, long-term commitments due to their exposure to instability.

Impact on Self-Esteem and Emotional Stability
Children growing up in unstable environments may internalize feelings of worthlessness or inadequacy. Constantly witnessing relationships that fail or dissolve can lead them to believe they are unworthy of love and stability, thus affecting their self-esteem. This emotional instability may become ingrained in their psyche, leading to struggles with anxiety and depression as they grow older.

A sense of security is crucial for emotional development; without it, children may be unable to trust others or form meaningful attachments. As they age, this can hinder their ability to develop romantic relationships or even maintain friendships, as their fear of abandonment may drive them to avoid intimacy or emotional vulnerability. Their childhood experiences can create a deep-rooted belief that relationships are inherently unreliable and fleeting, mirroring the instability they grew up with.

Low self-esteem can also manifest in other areas of a child's life, such as academic performance or personal ambitions. Children who internalize negative beliefs about their worth may be less likely to pursue opportunities or challenge themselves, fearing failure or rejection. This lack of confidence can stifle their potential and prevent them from reaching important personal and professional milestones. Over time, these feelings of inadequacy can become a self-fulfilling prophecy, limiting their achievements and reinforcing their belief that they are undeserving of success.

Fear of Intimacy and Commitment Issues
As children mature into adults, the instability they experienced in childhood can translate into an intense fear of intimacy and commitment. Having witnessed a pattern of short-lived relationships, they may develop a protective barrier, avoiding closeness to prevent the emotional pain of potential loss. This

avoidance can manifest as commitment issues in romantic relationships, where they either avoid forming deep connections or sabotage relationships as a means of self-preservation.

For some, the emotional detachment they adopt as a coping mechanism in childhood can carry into their adult lives. This detachment may serve as a temporary way to cope with their feelings of insecurity and abandonment. Still, it ultimately prevents them from forming the deep, trusting relationships needed for emotional fulfillment. Their fear of vulnerability becomes a significant barrier to emotional connection, making it difficult for them to build lasting, healthy partnerships.

Additionally, individuals who grow up with an unstable relationship model may struggle with conflicting desires—longing for connection while simultaneously fearing it. They may enter into relationships but pull away when emotionally exposed or vulnerable. This push-and-pull dynamic can create an unhealthy cycle of relationships where they can never fully commit or invest in their partner. Ultimately, their fear of intimacy stems from a deep-seated belief that emotional closeness will inevitably lead to pain and disappointment.

Social Struggles and Isolation
Frequent partner introductions can also lead to difficulties in forming and maintaining social

relationships outside the home. Children in unstable environments may feel different from their peers, particularly if they compare their chaotic family life to friends with more stable households. This sense of difference can lead to feelings of isolation, making it harder for them to relate to others or feel accepted.

Additionally, children raised in unstable homes may develop a heightened awareness of their family's dysfunction, leading them to withdraw socially or avoid discussing their home life with others. This social withdrawal can further impact their ability to develop and sustain friendships, leaving them disconnected and unsupported in their social and emotional lives.

Social skills are often learned through observation and practice, but children who grow up in environments with unpredictable relationships may struggle to embrace them effectively. They may struggle to read social cues or trust others enough to build meaningful friendships. The fear of being judged or rejected by peers may lead them to keep others at a distance, ultimately resulting in social isolation. This isolation can have far-reaching consequences, affecting their friendships, future work relationships, and support networks. Without strong social connections, children may struggle to navigate challenges in adulthood, as they lack the support and sense of belonging from having trusted friends and allies. Encouraging positive peer interactions and helping children develop their social skills is crucial for mitigating these long-term effects.

Manifestation of Anxiety and Depression

The long-term psychological consequences of instability often manifest as chronic anxiety or depression. Children exposed to frequent partner changes may grow up with a pervasive sense of unpredictability, leading to feelings of constant worry or dread. This anxiety can be triggered by the fear of future instability in their relationships, as they may expect that all bonds will eventually break, just as they witnessed in their childhood. Depression can also take root in children who feel emotionally neglected or abandoned by their parents. A lack of emotional support during critical developmental stages may leave them feeling unloved or forgotten, which can contribute to a deep sense of sadness and hopelessness that follows them into adulthood.

The unpredictability of their home environment can also lead to hyper-vigilance. Children may constantly be on edge, anticipating the next disruption or change. This state of heightened alertness can make it difficult for them to relax or enjoy the present moment, leading to chronic stress. Over time, this can take a toll on their mental and physical health, contributing to sleep disturbances, fatigue, and other stress-related ailments.

For children who internalize these feelings, the world can become inherently unsafe and unpredictable. This worldview can lead to a negative outlook on life, where hope and optimism are replaced by fear and uncertainty. Such children may struggle to find joy in everyday activities, and feelings of helplessness may overshadow their sense of purpose. Addressing these issues early through supportive interventions is crucial to preventing long-term psychological harm.

The Importance of Parental Communication and Stability

Parental communication and stability are vital to mitigating the adverse effects of frequent partner introductions. Children need reassurance that they remain a priority in their parents' lives, even when new relationships develop. Parents can help minimize feelings of insecurity and abandonment by maintaining consistent routines and providing emotional support. It is essential to introduce new partners only after establishing a serious commitment. This prevents children from becoming emotionally invested in a relationship that may not last, which can protect them from additional emotional harm. Parents should be mindful of how their dating choices affect their children's emotional well-being and strive to provide an environment that fosters security and trust. Clear and open communication is crucial in helping children navigate changes in their family dynamic. Parents should take the time to explain their new relationship in age-appropriate terms, addressing any questions or concerns the child may have. Children need to understand that they are not being replaced and that their place in the family remains secure. This reassurance helps build resilience and fosters a sense of belonging, even when the family structure evolves.

Additionally, maintaining traditions and routines can provide children with a sense of continuity, even during times of change. Whether family dinners, bedtime rituals, or weekend outings, these consistent activities help children feel grounded and remind them that they are part of a stable and loving family unit. Parents should also prioritize quality one-on-one time with each child, reinforcing their importance and meeting their emotional needs.

Seeking Professional Guidance
In cases where a child's emotional distress becomes pronounced, seeking professional guidance is highly recommended. A therapist or counselor can provide valuable support, helping the child process their emotions and develop healthier coping mechanisms. Professional intervention can be especially beneficial for children exhibiting signs of anxiety, depression, or social withdrawal, as it offers them a safe space to express their feelings and begin to heal from the emotional wounds caused by family instability.

Interview with a Family Therapist

Dr. Jane Doe, a family therapist, emphasizes the importance of stability for children in single-parent homes. "Introducing new partners too quickly can disrupt a child's sense of safety," she explains. "Children need time to build trust, and parents should respect this need by taking things slowly." Dr. Doe suggests waiting six months to a year before bringing a new partner into the home, allowing time for the child and the partner to adjust.

Dr. Doe elaborates that children in single-parent homes often experience heightened anxiety when faced with new family dynamics. "It's crucial to remember that children are not just adjusting to the new person; they're also navigating their own emotions and trying to understand what these changes mean for their relationship with their parent," she says. "The introduction of a new partner can make a child feel as though their bond with their parent is being threatened, which can lead to feelings of insecurity or even resentment."

She also stresses the importance of open communication throughout the process. "Parents should be upfront with their children about their intentions while also being sensitive to their child's feelings. It's important to give children a voice in the process, allowing them to express their concerns or fears without fear of reprimand," Dr. Doe advises. "Parents can help alleviate some of the anxiety that comes with change by including children in age-appropriate conversations."

Dr. Doe further suggests that parents engage in regular family activities to maintain a sense of normalcy and continuity during transition periods. "Consistent routines provide a comforting anchor for children, especially when other aspects of their lives change. These routines can provide security, whether having a family movie night, cooking dinner together, or maintaining bedtime rituals."

She also highlights the role of the new partner in building trust with the child. "The new partner should take the time to get to know the child and slowly respect their boundaries. Rushing the relationship can lead to resistance and emotional withdrawal. Instead, the partner should focus on developing a genuine connection by engaging in activities the child enjoys and showing interest in their hobbies. This approach helps the child see the partner as an ally, not a threat."

Dr. Doe emphasizes that every family is unique, and there is no one-size-fits-all solution. "The key is to be patient and empathetic. It's about understanding the child's perspective and ensuring that the child feels loved, heard, and secure, even as the family dynamic changes.

Family therapy can also be an effective tool for addressing the impact of instability on the entire family unit. By involving parents and children, family therapy provides a platform for open communication, allowing each member to express their feelings and work toward a more cohesive, supportive dynamic. It can also help parents better understand how their actions affect their children and provide them with strategies for creating a more stable home environment.

Early intervention is vital to mitigating the long-term effects of instability. By addressing emotional and behavioral issues as soon as they arise, parents can help their children build resilience and develop the skills to navigate future challenges. Professional support can give children the tools needed to cope with difficult emotions, build self-esteem, and establish healthy relationships as they grow older.

Conclusion

The long-term psychological effects of frequent partner introductions are profound and far-reaching. From struggles with self-esteem and emotional detachment to fear of intimacy and social isolation, children exposed to relationship instability face significant challenges as they grow into adulthood. However, by prioritizing stability, open communication, and emotional support, parents can help mitigate these adverse effects and provide their children with the tools they need to build healthier, more fulfilling relationships.

Creating a stable and supportive environment requires intentionality and a deep understanding of a child's emotional needs. By putting their well-being first, parents can help their children develop positive self-worth, build trusting relationships, and confidently navigate life. While the challenges of modern family dynamics are complex, a commitment to fostering security, trust, and love within the home can make all the difference in a child's long-term psychological health.

Chapter 4

Age-Based Reactions to Relationship Instability

Children's reactions to frequent partner introductions vary significantly depending on their age and developmental stage. Understanding these differences is crucial for single parents navigating new relationships, helping them minimize emotional damage and foster healthier family dynamics.

Reactions in Young Children (Infancy to Early Childhood)

Young children are highly vulnerable to instability. Their emotional security relies on stable, consistent caregivers. When new "mother" or "father" figures frequently come and go, it disrupts their ability to form secure attachments, which are vital for healthy emotional and social development. These children are still in the early stages of learning to trust and bond with caregivers, so frequent changes can leave them confused, anxious, and insecure.

Young children in unstable environments may experience emotional regression or display signs of distress, such as increased clinginess, bedwetting, or tantrums. Their inability to understand the complexities of relationships makes them particularly sensitive to the revolving door of adult figures. Over time, this instability can stunt their ability to form meaningful, trusting relationships in the future. Without a strong foundation of attachment, they may grow up with deep-seated fears of abandonment, making it difficult for them to navigate relationships later in life.

Young children often thrive on routine and predictability. The presence of a new partner can alter their daily routines, further contributing to their sense of confusion and insecurity. For instance, bedtime routines or mealtimes may change if a new adult becomes involved, making it harder for the child to adjust. Parents should strive to maintain consistency in their children's daily routines, reassuring them that their needs will always be met despite changes.

Parents may need to realize the full impact of their romantic decisions on their young children because the effects can often be subtle. However, the underlying anxiety and instability caused by frequent partner introductions can have long-term consequences on the child's emotional health and ability to trust others. To mitigate this, parents should prioritize consistency in their relationships and ensure the child's place in the family is secure no matter what changes happen. Creating a stable environment where the child knows what to expect daily can foster a greater sense of security and resilience.

Reactions in School-Age Children

As children enter school, they become more aware of their family's structure and may begin to compare it to that of their peers. Frequent partner changes can cause confusion and embarrassment, particularly if children feel their home life differs from the stability they perceive in others' families.

At this age, children may experience jealousy, especially if they feel their new partner is taking away their parents' attention. They might act out at school or home, displaying behavioral issues such as defiance, withdrawal, or difficulty concentrating in school. These children are still developing their social and emotional intelligence, and the instability of constantly changing relationships may cause them to struggle with forming peer relationships.

School-age children may also distrust new partners, question their intentions, and feel protective of their relationship with their parents. This skepticism can lead to emotional distancing from the new partner, challenging the development of meaningful bonds. The lack of stability also affects the child's ability to trust others outside the home, leading to social difficulties and challenges in forming friendships.

Their understanding of authority can also become strained. Introducing a new adult who assumes an authoritative role without building trust can lead to resentment and rebellion. This development phase is critical for forming a healthy sense of self and emotional regulation. When disrupted, it can have far-reaching effects on their ability to build healthy relationships and cope with emotions as they mature.

Parents of school-age children should communicate openly and honestly about family changes, ensuring that children feel heard and understood. Maintaining consistent routines and boundaries, regardless of the presence of a new partner, will help the child feel more secure. Parents should also be prepared to answer any questions their child might have about the new relationship in a way that reassures them of their place within the family. By involving the child in discussions and acknowledging their feelings, parents can foster a greater sense of stability and acceptance.

Reactions in Adolescents (Teenagers)
Adolescents are more emotionally mature and have a deeper understanding of relationships, but this doesn't mean they are less affected by frequent partner changes. Teenagers are often more critical and cynical about their parents' romantic decisions. They may become suspicious or resentful of new partners, especially if they perceive the relationships as short-lived or unstable.

Teenagers may feel a loss of control in a household where adult figures frequently change, leading them to assert their independence through rebellion or risky behaviors. They may also question their parents' judgment, straining the parent-child relationship. This emotional disconnection can further lead teenagers to distance themselves from the family. Some may even reject the idea of close, long-term relationships, having witnessed instability throughout their formative years.

Adolescents are at a stage where their peer relationships play a significant role in their self-identity. Teenagers may struggle with embarrassment or isolation when their home life is unstable, especially if they think their family lives differ from their friends' more stable homes. This insecurity can negatively impact their social interactions, leaving them feeling different or "ostracized" by their peers.

Case Study 3: Malik, Age 11

> Malik's mother, recently divorced, struggled with the challenges of being a single parent. The emotional toll of the divorce, combined with the pressure of raising her son alone, led her to seek companionship, and she began dating again. Over a short period, Malik was introduced to several new figures, each of whom seemed to play a significant role in his life, only to disappear just as quickly. This

cycle left Malik feeling confused, abandoned, and emotionally vulnerable.

Malik tried to form a connection each time a new partner entered their lives. He craved stability and wanted to feel that there were supportive adults around him, especially after the loss of his father figure through the divorce. However, each time the relationship ended, Malik felt even more disconnected and unsure of his place in his mother's life. The repeated pattern of forming and losing connections caused Malik to internalize the belief that relationships were inherently unstable and temporary. The impact on Malik's emotional well-being soon became evident. His once energetic and curious demeanor began to fade, replaced by withdrawal and sadness. Malik's grades at school slipped as he struggled to concentrate, and his teachers noticed a significant change in his behavior. He became more reserved, avoiding interactions with both peers and teachers. Malik also began refusing to participate in activities he used to enjoy, like soccer and drawing, as his motivation waned under the weight of his emotional confusion.

Malik's mother, preoccupied with her emotional struggles, initially didn't realize the full extent of her son's distress. She believed introducing new people into their lives would help them move forward from the divorce, but she hadn't considered how these rapid changes might affect Malik's sense of security. It wasn't until Malik's teacher requested a meeting to discuss his declining performance and visible signs of anxiety that she realized the severity of the situation.

Determined to make a change, Malik's mother put her dating life on hold to prioritize her son's emotional needs. She recognized that Malik needed stability and consistent support to regain his sense of security. She began spending more quality one-on-one time with Malik, engaging in activities they enjoyed, like visiting the park, playing board games, and cooking meals together. These moments helped Malik feel more connected to his mother, reminding him he was her top priority.

In addition to dedicating more time to Malik, his mother enrolled him in a mentorship program. The program paired Malik with a stable male role model who could provide guidance, support, and consistency—something lacking since the divorce. Malik's mentor, Mr. Johnson, was a kind and patient figure who took the time to build a genuine connection with him. They would meet weekly, engaging in hiking, building model cars, and discussing Malik's interests and aspirations. Through these interactions, Malik developed a sense of trust and stability that had been missing from his life.

Mr. Johnson's consistent presence reassured Malik that not all relationships were temporary. Having a stable male figure who showed up week after week helped Malik rebuild his confidence and trust in adults. During their sessions, Malik began to open up, sharing his fears about people leaving and his struggles at school. Mr. Johnson listened attentively, validating Malik's feelings and offering him the emotional support he desperately needed. This mentorship became a turning point in Malik's journey toward emotional recovery.

With time, Malik's mood and performance at school slowly began to improve. The anxiety that had plagued him started to subside as he felt more secure in his environment. He began participating in class again, and his teachers noted that he seemed more engaged and willing to interact with his peers. Malik even returned to playing soccer, finding joy in his once-loved sport. The stability provided by his mother's renewed focus on his well-being, combined with the positive influence of his mentor, helped Malik regain a sense of normalcy.

This case study highlights the profound impact of relationship instability on a child's emotional and psychological well-being. Malik's story underscores the importance of providing children with stability, especially during times of significant change. Frequent introductions of new partners can leave children feeling insecure and unsure of their place in the family. By recognizing Malik's needs and making intentional changes, his mother created an environment where Malik could thrive once again.

Parents in similar situations can learn from Malik's experience. When navigating new relationships, it is crucial to consider children's emotional needs. Stability, consistency, and the presence of supportive role models can significantly affect a child's ability to cope with change. By prioritizing their child's emotional health and providing a secure environment, parents can help their children build resilience and regain their confidence, even under challenging transitions.

Furthermore, adolescents may feel pressured to form alliances with or against new partners. This creates complicated family dynamics, as teens may feel caught between loyalty to their parents and feelings about the new partner. Navigating these conflicting emotions can result in heightened family tensions, which, if not addressed, can leave lasting emotional scars. Adolescents may also resent it if they perceive their parent prioritizes the new partner over their needs, leading to emotional disconnection and distrust.

Parents should support their adolescent children by involving them in conversations about relationship changes and respecting their feelings and concerns. Giving teenagers a sense of agency and validating their perspectives can help reduce resentment and create a more harmonious transition when introducing a new partner. They must also acknowledge that adolescents have evolving views on relationships and use this as an opportunity for meaningful discussions about healthy partnerships, boundaries, and respect. Parents should also be mindful of the example they set for their teenagers. Adolescents are highly impressionable, and how they observe their parents managing relationships will significantly influence their future romantic decisions. Demonstrating respectful communication, mutual understanding, and emotional maturity can give teenagers a positive model of healthy relationships.

Conclusion: Navigating Relationship Instability by Age Group

Each age group reacts differently to relationship instability, and understanding these unique responses is essential for parents. Younger children need reassurance and consistency to foster secure attachments, while school-age children and adolescents require more open communication and emotional support. By prioritizing their child's emotional well-being and providing a stable, loving environment, even in the face of family changes, parents can minimize the harmful effects of frequent partner introductions and help their children develop healthy relationships and emotional resilience.

Parents should be mindful of their children's emotional needs at different stages of development, understanding that their actions significantly impact their children's sense of security and well-being. By maintaining consistency, fostering open dialogue, and involving children in decisions that affect the family, parents can navigate the complexities of modern relationships to minimize harm and promote a supportive, nurturing environment.

In the long term, children who experience a stable, loving environment are more likely to develop into emotionally resilient adults capable of forming healthy relationships. By considering their children's developmental needs and adjusting their approach accordingly, parents can help mitigate the challenges of relationship instability and set the foundation for a healthier future for their children.

Chapter 5

Trust in Authority and Discipline

Introducing new partners into a child's life affects their sense of family stability and significantly impacts how they view authority figures and discipline. When a non-parental adult assumes the role of disciplinarian, it can create confusion for the child, especially if the partner's approach to discipline conflicts with that of the parent. This can erode the child's trust in both the parent and other authority figures, leading to emotional instability and behavioral issues.

The Confusion of Multiple Authority Figures

Children thrive when they understand their actions' boundaries and consequences. However, when multiple adults with varying disciplinary styles are involved, children can become confused and unsure about acceptable behavior. For example, a child might receive strict consequences from a new partner for behavior that previously went unaddressed or was handled more leniently by the parent. This inconsistency disrupts the child's ability to navigate household rules, leading to frustration and rebellion.

Children may sometimes feel that the new partner's authority is illegitimate, especially if they view them as outsiders. This can foster resentment, mainly if the partner enforces rules in a manner that seems unfair or overbearing. The child may question the parent's judgment in allowing someone else to discipline them, leading to a breakdown in trust and respect for authority figures in general. They often view their primary caregiver as their central source of stability. When a new partner takes on an authoritative role without establishing a trusting relationship with the child, it can create a feeling of instability. The child may perceive that their parent is giving away authority to someone they barely know, which can make the child feel vulnerable and uncertain about where they stand within the family structure. This uncertainty can lead to a sense of helplessness, further fueling resistance to the new partner's role.

Eroding Trust Through Inconsistent Discipline
One of the most damaging effects of inconsistent discipline is the erosion of trust between the child and the parent. When a parent allows a new partner to take on a disciplinary role too soon or without clear boundaries, the child may feel betrayed or neglected. This is particularly true if the child is still adjusting to the new family dynamics. By granting authority to someone who hasn't yet earned the child's trust, the parent risks undermining the security and emotional foundation they've built. Children may also struggle

with favoritism or jealousy if they perceive the parent as prioritizing the partner's authority over their relationship with the child. This perception can foster a sense of alienation, where the child feels like they no longer have a place of importance in the family. The resulting emotional turmoil can manifest in defiance, withdrawal, or rebellion as the child seeks to reclaim control when they feel powerless. The sense of betrayal that comes from inconsistent discipline can also affect the child's future relationships with authority figures outside the home. For example, a child who feels that their voice has been dismissed or that discipline has been unfair may carry those feelings into their relationships with teachers, coaches, and other adults. This erosion of trust can have long-term consequences, making it difficult for the child to form respectful and trusting connections with authority figures.

The Importance of Consistency and Clear Boundaries

For discipline to be practical and maintain the child's trust, it must be consistent and clearly defined. The child's parents should be the primary disciplinarians, particularly in the early stages of introducing a new partner. This consistency reassures the child that their parent remains their emotional anchor despite changes in the family dynamic. Parents should communicate clear boundaries to the new partner, outlining what role, if any, they will play in disciplining the child. It is crucial to allow the child time to build trust with the new partner before they take on any disciplinary role. This gradual process allows the child to adjust to the new family dynamic without feeling overwhelmed or threatened. It also helps the child understand that while the partner is part of the family, the parent remains the primary authority figure. Setting clear and consistent rules within the household is crucial in avoiding confusion. The child should know that the exact expectations apply, regardless of who is present. Parents can converse with the new partner and the child about the household rules, ensuring everyone is on the same page. This collaborative approach can help the child feel more secure and reduce the likelihood of resentment.

Respecting the Child's Emotional Development
: A child's ability to navigate relationships and authority is directly tied to emotional growth. A parent allowing a new partner to assume disciplinary responsibilities too soon can disrupt the child's emotional development, mainly if their voice or feelings are dismissed. Children need to feel heard and valued, especially during periods of transition. A rushed or inconsistent approach to discipline can hinder their ability to form healthy relationships with authority figures inside and outside the home. Moreover, a new partner's involvement in discipline should be introduced with sensitivity and care,

considering the child's age, temperament, and individual needs. Children are more likely to accept their partner's authority if they feel respected and if the partner takes the time to build a relationship based on trust and mutual understanding.

When children feel that their emotional needs are being overlooked, they may internalize a sense of unimportance, affecting their self-esteem and emotional well-being. Parents need to prioritize their children's feelings and work toward building an inclusive family environment where the children's opinions and emotions are valued. Introducing discipline from a new partner should always be framed within the context of care and support rather than authority and control.

The Role of the New Partner in Building Trust
The new partner's role in establishing trust before taking on any disciplinary responsibilities cannot be overstated. Trust-building activities such as spending quality time together, participating in shared interests, and creating joyous memories are essential for developing a solid foundation. These activities can help the child see the partner as genuinely caring for them rather than simply an authority figure. Patience is a vital component during this period. The new partner should avoid making any disciplinary decisions until a level of trust has been established. Instead, they can support the parent in enforcing established rules by offering encouragement and

positive reinforcement, which helps build credibility without overstepping boundaries. Demonstrating empathy and respect for the child's feelings goes a long way in fostering a positive relationship that eventually allows for a more effective disciplinary role if and when it is appropriate.

Children are more receptive to discipline from adults they trust and respect. By building a connection based on empathy, understanding, and shared experiences, the new partner can gradually transition into a supportive role in maintaining household rules. The partner must also recognize that every child is different; what works in one situation may not work in another. Flexibility and adaptability are vital qualities in a new partner trying to integrate into an established family structure.

Supporting Emotional Security Through Discipline

The goal of discipline should always be to support the child's emotional security and development, not just to enforce rules. A consistent and thoughtful approach to discipline ensures that the child feels safe and supported, even in the face of change. By maintaining clear boundaries and prioritizing the parent-child relationship, single parents can help their children develop a healthy respect for authority without feeling threatened by introducing a new partner.

Parents should also use discipline as an opportunity to teach problem-solving skills and emotional regulation. Instead of focusing solely on punitive measures, discipline should involve conversations about the child's behavior, its reasons, and potential solutions. This approach encourages the child to reflect on their actions and understand the consequences, fostering emotional intelligence and resilience. The new partner can play a supportive role by positively reinforcing these lessons. For example, rather than issuing consequences, they can help guide the child through problem-solving processes, offering suggestions and encouragement. This reinforces that discipline is about growth and learning rather than punishment, which can significantly improve the child's perception of discipline and authority figures.

Building Trust and Stability in Blended Families
Regarding discipline and new partners, patience, communication, and respect are essential. Children need time to adjust to new dynamics and to understand that their relationship with their parents remains intact. By focusing on consistency, respect, and trust-building, single parents can navigate the complexities of discipline in blended families without compromising their child's emotional well-being.

Parents must recognize the impact of new relationships on their children's perception of authority and discipline. When intentionally introducing new partners and gradually integrating them into the family's disciplinary framework, parents can help their children feel more secure and valued. The ultimate goal is to create a stable, supportive environment where discipline is consistent, boundaries are clear, and the child's emotional growth is prioritized. Blended families can thrive when all members feel respected, valued, and secure. By approaching discipline thoughtfully, allowing time for trust to develop, and maintaining open lines of communication, parents and new partners can work together to build a cohesive family dynamic that supports the well-being of every member.

Chapter 6

Secure Attachments and Future Commitments

Secure attachments are vital to a child's emotional and social well-being, providing the foundation for trusting relationships. A child's first attachment experiences with their primary caregivers set the tone for how they relate to others in adulthood. However, frequent introductions of new partners can severely disrupt the formation of these essential bonds, particularly in young children who rely on stability to feel safe and secure.

Children thrive with consistent, nurturing caregivers who provide a predictable emotional environment. When exposed to transient relationships—where partners come and go—the child's attachment process is interrupted, leading to feelings of confusion, insecurity, and mistrust. This disruption can have profound long-term consequences, manifesting as difficulty forming deep, trusting relationships in adulthood. Without stable attachments, children may struggle with feelings of abandonment, which can lead them to avoid relationships altogether or approach them with skepticism, assuming that relationships are inherently unstable and destined to fail.

The Impact of Transient Relationships on Secure Attachment Formation

Secure attachment begins in infancy, with a child relying on a consistent caregiver to meet their emotional and physical needs. Over time, this consistency allows the child to feel safe, secure, and loved. However, this process is disrupted when new partners are frequently introduced into the child's life. Young children, in particular, cannot understand why adults come and go. They may form tentative attachments to the new partner, only to experience confusion and emotional pain when that partner leaves. The emotional toll of this cycle is significant. A child exposed to transient relationships may begin to view relationships as temporary and unstable. The fear of abandonment becomes ingrained, and the child may struggle with trust and become wary of forming new relationships in the future. This cycle of unstable attachments can hinder emotional development and create barriers to forming long-lasting bonds later in life, both romantically and socially.

Children who experience frequent changes in caregivers may also become hyper-vigilant, constantly bracing themselves for the next departure.

This constant state of anxiety can hinder their ability to relax and form healthy connections. It can also lead to behaviors aimed at self-preservation, such as emotional withdrawal or acting out, which are coping mechanisms developed to deal with the unpredictable nature of their environment.

Fear of Commitment in Adolescence and Adulthood

As children grow older, the instability they experienced during their formative years often translates into a fear of commitment in adolescence and adulthood. Teens who have witnessed their parents' relationships repeatedly fail may develop a cynical view of love and long-term partnerships. They may enter relationships with the expectation that they will inevitably end, mirroring the instability they witnessed in their early years. This fear of commitment can manifest in several ways—some may avoid relationships entirely, while others may sabotage their connections, consciously or unconsciously, to protect themselves from potential rejection.

This pattern of avoidance or distrust can have far-reaching consequences. Romantic relationships may prevent individuals from experiencing the depth of connection necessary for long-term emotional fulfillment. It can also hinder their ability to maintain close friendships or professional relationships, limiting their social support network. A child who grows up fearing commitment may also have difficulty setting boundaries, as they may struggle to understand what a healthy relationship entails. They might either become overly attached, fearing abandonment, or keep an emotional distance to protect themselves from being hurt. Both scenarios can prevent them from experiencing the kind of supportive, trusting relationships that are crucial for emotional well-being.

The Importance of Consistent, Nurturing Relationships

The foundation for healthy emotional development is built through consistent, nurturing relationships in childhood. Children who experience reliable, loving caregivers are more likely to develop emotional resilience and the ability to form secure attachments. In contrast, children who grow up in environments of inconsistency—where adults frequently come and go—are often left feeling insecure and emotionally unsupported. The lack of stable attachment figures deprives them of the emotional blueprint to navigate future relationships successfully.

To foster healthy attachments, single parents must be mindful of how frequently they introduce new partners to their children. While dating and forming new relationships are natural, it is essential to ensure that the introduction of a partner is deliberate and thoughtful. Introducing new partners only after a serious commitment has been established can help mitigate the negative impact on the child's attachment process. Parents must also remain attuned to their child's emotional state throughout the process, providing reassurance and maintaining open lines of communication.

In addition to delaying introductions until a relationship is serious, parents should also focus on nurturing their existing bond with their child. Consistent emotional availability and engagement are vital to helping children feel secure. This includes spending quality time together, actively listening to their concerns, and providing comfort during times of stress. By demonstrating consistent care and attention, parents can help build a secure attachment that will serve as a protective factor against the challenges of transient relationships.

Building a Path Forward for the Child's Emotional Health

Building secure attachments after experiencing instability requires effort and intentionality. Parents can create a stable home environment with predictable routines, rules, and relationships. Even if a new partner is introduced, it is crucial to ensure that the child's needs are prioritized and their sense of security remains intact. Providing consistent emotional support and reinforcing the child's importance within the family structure can help repair the feeling of trust that previous disruptions may have damaged.

Predictability is critical to establishing a sense of security. Daily routines—consistent meal times, bedtime rituals, and regular family activities—can provide a comforting structure that helps children feel grounded. These routines reassure children that certain aspects of their lives remain stable, even when other parts change. Professional support may be necessary for children who have experienced significant instability. Therapy can help them process their feelings of abandonment or mistrust and guide them in developing healthier emotional coping mechanisms. Parents can also model healthy relationships by demonstrating open communication, mutual respect, and emotional consistency with their new partner. By doing so, they provide their children with the tools they need to form secure attachments in the future.

Therapists can also help children develop emotional regulation skills, which can be particularly helpful for those who have experienced instability. These skills help children effectively identify and manage their emotions, reducing anxiety and fostering healthier interpersonal relationships. Family therapy can also provide a safe space for parents and children to work through their feelings and strengthen their bond. Parents should also prioritize their emotional health. Children are highly perceptive, and if they sense that a parent is emotionally unstable, it can heighten their insecurities. By seeking support through counseling or support groups, parents can model the importance of emotional well-being and demonstrate resilience, providing a positive example for their children.

Conclusion

The frequent introduction of new partners into a child's life can have far-reaching consequences, particularly when forming secure attachments and navigating future commitments. Children rely on stable, nurturing relationships to build the emotional resilience necessary for healthy social development. This process is disrupted when exposed to transient relationships, leading to long-term trust issues and a fear of commitment. By prioritizing stability, thoughtful introductions of new partners, and maintaining consistent emotional support, single parents can help mitigate the negative impact of these changes on their child's emotional health. Providing children with a stable emotional foundation sets them up for success in forming deep, meaningful connections throughout their lives and personal and professional relationships.

Fostering secure attachments creates an environment where children feel safe, valued, and supported. By being mindful of the potential challenges and addressing them with care, parents can nurture their children's emotional growth, ensuring that they have the resilience and confidence needed to build healthy, fulfilling relationships in the future.

Chapter 7

The Reactions to Family Structure

Building healthy family dynamics requires consistent effort, open communication, and long-term strategies that can adapt to changing needs over time. Families are unique, and what works for one might not work for another. However, there are common approaches that can help cultivate a nurturing environment for all members, enabling them to thrive individually and as a cohesive unit.

1. Prioritize Quality Time Together

Spending quality time together strengthens bonds and creates a sense of belonging. Activities like family meals, game nights, weekend outings, or simply having discussions without distractions can foster a sense of unity. Making family time a non-negotiable priority demonstrates that each member is valued and creates opportunities for positive interactions and deeper connections.

Quality time can be simple and inexpensive. Simple activities like cooking together, gardening, or walking in the neighborhood can be as meaningful.

The key is to be fully present—putting away phones, turning off the TV, and focusing on each other. Families can build strong memories that last a lifetime by creating consistent routines for spending time together.

2. Practice Open and Honest Communication

Effective communication is the cornerstone of healthy relationships. Encourage every family member to express their feelings, thoughts, and concerns without fear of judgment or retribution. Active listening is vital— when one person speaks, others should listen attentively, showing empathy and respect. Setting aside regular times to discuss issues openly and celebrate successes as a family builds trust and understanding.

To foster open communication, create a safe space where everyone feels heard. This can be as simple as a weekly family meeting or a daily check-in. Encourage children to articulate their emotions by using "I feel" statements, which helps them communicate effectively without placing blame. By validating each other's experiences and feelings, families can strengthen their emotional bonds and promote a culture of openness.

3. Set Clear Boundaries and Roles

Healthy boundaries and defined roles provide structure and security. Each member should understand their responsibilities within the family while knowing their personal space and autonomy are respected. Establishing boundaries helps prevent misunderstandings and conflicts, while clearly defined roles ensure everyone contributes meaningfully through chores, emotional support, or shared decision-making.

Boundaries should be flexible enough to adapt to changing needs. For example, as children grow older, their roles and responsibilities may shift, requiring parents to adjust expectations accordingly. Open discussions about boundaries help ensure everyone is comfortable and understands their role in maintaining a harmonious household. Respecting each other's privacy and individuality is vital to fostering a supportive environment.

4. Embrace Conflict Resolution

Conflicts are natural in any relationship, and families are no exception. Embracing healthy conflict resolution means approaching disagreements with a problem-solving mindset instead of avoiding or escalating them. Teach children to express their disagreements respectfully and model how to negotiate and find common ground. Learning to resolve conflicts constructively strengthens family bonds and reduces resentment.

When conflicts arise, it is essential to stay calm and focus on the issue rather than the person. Use "I" statements to express feelings without blaming others, and encourage family members to listen actively to one another's perspectives. Families can also benefit from establishing ground rules for resolving conflicts, such as taking turns speaking and avoiding interrupting. Families can grow stronger and more resilient by working together to find mutually acceptable solutions.

5. Foster Emotional Intelligence and Empathy

Encouraging emotional intelligence—the ability to identify, understand, and manage emotions—is vital for building healthy family dynamics. Parents and caregivers should model empathy, helping children understand and validate their feelings and those of others. Family members who practice empathy can better support each other, fostering a more caring and nurturing environment.

To cultivate emotional intelligence, teach children to recognize and name their emotions. Please encourage them to think about how others might feel in different situations, which can help them develop empathy. Modeling empathy as a parent—by acknowledging and validating your child's emotions—sets a powerful example. Emotional intelligence helps family relationships and equips children with skills to navigate social situations outside the home.

6. Encourage Individual Growth and Autonomy

While family unity is essential, it is equally vital to recognize and support each member's individuality.

Encourage hobbies, passions, and personal goals, and celebrate achievements, big or small. Allowing space for individual growth helps each family member develop a strong sense of self, ultimately contributing to a healthier family dynamic.

Supporting individual growth means recognizing that each family member has unique strengths, interests, and aspirations. Parents can encourage autonomy by allowing children to make age-appropriate decisions and take on new challenges. This helps children build confidence and independence. Celebrating each member's successes—whether a school achievement, a work promotion, or a personal milestone—reinforces the importance of personal growth within the family context.

7. Create Family Rituals and Traditions
Rituals and traditions help create lasting memories, giving families something to look forward to, which can strengthen connections. Whether it's celebrating birthdays in a particular way, seasonal traditions, or small daily rituals like bedtime stories, these moments build a shared family identity that brings comfort and joy.

These rituals or special occasions don't have to be elaborate—consistency and meaning matter. For example, having a special dinner every Friday night or an annual family trip can create cherished memories. Traditions provide a sense of continuity, especially during change or stress. They also remind the family of its values and the importance of spending time together, reinforcing the bonds that hold the family together.

8. Model Healthy Relationships

Children learn about relationships by observing the adults around them. Demonstrating respect, love, and support in your relationships—whether with a partner, friends, or extended family—sets a powerful example. Treat others with kindness, communicate effectively, and demonstrate problem-solving skills to help children understand healthy relationships. Modeling healthy relationships also involves showing how to manage disagreements constructively. Let children see that conflict is a normal part of relationships and can be resolved through respectful dialogue. Show affection and appreciation for your partner or other family members, and make an effort to involve children in activities that promote positive interactions. Children learn how to build and maintain positive connections by witnessing healthy relationships.

9. Foster a Culture of Gratitude and Positivity

A culture of gratitude within the family can have a significant positive impact. Encourage family members to share things they are grateful for regularly. Emphasizing positivity and celebrating small victories can help family members stay resilient through difficult times, providing a sense of optimism and security.

One way to foster gratitude is to create a family gratitude ritual, such as sharing one thing you're thankful for during dinner or before bedtime. Practicing gratitude helps shift the focus away from problems and toward the positive aspects of life. Celebrating achievements—no matter how small—reinforces a positive mindset and helps family members feel appreciated. This positivity can be a powerful tool for coping with challenges and maintaining a supportive family environment.

10. Seek Support When Needed

Recognizing when to seek outside help is an essential aspect of maintaining healthy family dynamics. Whether it's family counseling, support groups, or educational resources, seeking professional guidance shows strength, not weakness. It demonstrates a commitment to growth and well-being, which can positively influence the entire family. There is no shame in asking for help when challenges feel overwhelming. Family counseling can provide a neutral space for members to express their feelings and work through issues with the guidance of a trained professional. Support groups can also offer valuable insights and a sense of community for families facing similar challenges. By being proactive about seeking support, families can address issues before they escalate and continue to grow together in a healthy, positive way.

Building healthy family dynamics is a lifelong journey that requires flexibility, patience, and consistent effort. Families can create a supportive environment where every member feels valued and loved by nurturing communication, understanding, and respect.

Chapter 8

Strategies for Mitigating Negative Impacts

Despite the challenges, single parents can employ various strategies to minimize the emotional and psychological toll that frequent partner introductions can have on their children. Ensuring stability, clear communication, and emotional support is vital in helping children navigate these changes healthily.

Prioritize Emotional Readiness

Introducing a new partner into a child's life should be approached with care and forethought. It's essential to ensure that both the parent and the new partner fully commit to the relationship before involving the child. Jumping into introductions too early can cause confusion and insecurity. Parents must realize they aren't the only ones entering a new relationship—their child is, too. The child's emotional needs must be considered equally important to the romantic partner's role in the family dynamic. Parents should also reflect on their emotional readiness before introducing someone new. If a parent is still healing from a previous relationship or unsure about the new partner's long-term role in the family, rushing into introductions can destabilize the child. Children thrive in environments where they feel secure, and this security can only be built when the parent is clear about their emotional state and the future of the relationship. Parents must communicate this sense of stability to their children to avoid placing them in emotionally uncertain situations.

Introducing a new partner requires careful timing and understanding of the potential emotional impact on the child. Children often feel vulnerable during changes, and parents must be mindful not to introduce instability. Ensuring emotional readiness helps minimize confusion, reassures the child, and creates a foundation for healthy, positive relationships.

Open Communication

Maintaining honest and age-appropriate conversations about the new relationship is essential in ensuring children feel included and emotionally secure. Instead of keeping children in the dark about new relationships, parents should foster an open dialogue where children feel comfortable asking questions and expressing their feelings. Parents can explain new relationships in simple terms for younger children, helping them understand what changes, if any, might occur. The conversation can be more nuanced for older children or teenagers, allowing them to express concerns or reservations. The key is making sure that the child knows their emotions are valid and that they can speak openly about their experiences. Parents should actively listen and respond to the child's concerns, reinforcing that their place in the family remains secure regardless of changes in the parent's relationship status. Open communication can also help children adjust to the new partner more easily. Allowing the child to be part of the process, sharing updates, and providing clear explanations about the seriousness of the relationship all contribute to a smoother transition. This transparency can prevent feelings of shock or betrayal if a partner suddenly becomes a more prominent presence in the home.

When introducing a new partner, it's also beneficial to involve the child gradually, explaining why this person is important and how they will fit into the family. Clear and open communication helps the child feel informed and strengthens family trust, reducing potential resentment or insecurity.

Consistency in Routines and Discipline
Children need consistency, especially in times of change. Maintaining stable household routines and a consistent approach to discipline is crucial when introducing a new partner. Children used to a particular structure may become unsettled when routines change abruptly, such as when a new partner influences bedtimes, family activities, or house rules.

Even with the introduction of a new partner, maintaining established routines—whether meal times, bedtimes, or family traditions—helps children feel secure in their environment. A partner's presence shouldn't upend the rhythms that make children feel comfortable. Disruptions in these routines can cause stress, anxiety, and behavioral issues, as the child may struggle to adapt to changing expectations.

Discipline must also remain consistent. A new partner should wait to take on disciplinary roles, which can confuse the child or cause resentment. The parent should remain the primary authority figure, ensuring clear rules and boundaries. Any disciplinary role for the partner should be introduced gradually and only after the child has built a trusting relationship with them. Stability in discipline allows the child to feel safe and ensures that introducing a new partner does not create additional confusion or chaos in the household.

Additionally, consistency in routines and discipline gives children a sense of normalcy, even in the face of significant changes. It signals that the foundation of their home life remains intact despite new relationships, offering comfort and reassurance during transitions.

One-on-One Time with Your Child
One of the most effective ways to mitigate the emotional impact of a new relationship on your child

is by prioritizing one-on-one time with them. Children often feel neglected or displaced when a new partner demands the parent's attention. Ensuring you set aside dedicated time to spend with your child, you reaffirm their importance in your life. This time doesn't have to be elaborate. It can involve simple activities like walking, having dinner together, or engaging in a hobby the child enjoys. The goal is to let your child know that their relationship with you remains a top priority despite the changes in your romantic life. Quality time fosters security, reassures the child that they are valued, and helps to alleviate any fears they may have about being replaced. These one-on-one interactions allow you to check in with your child emotionally. During these moments, you can ask how they feel about the new partner and listen to any concerns. Open and supportive communication strengthens the parent-child bond, ensuring the child feels heard and understood. Spending one-on-one time also allows parents to monitor their children's emotional health more closely, providing a safe space to express their thoughts and feelings without fear of judgment. This individualized attention is critical for maintaining a strong parent-child connection amid family changes.

Supporting Emotional Transitions
It's essential to remember that every child will react differently to new relationships depending on their age, personality, and past experiences. Some children

may embrace a new partner quickly, while others might struggle with jealousy, resentment, or fear of abandonment. Parents should be patient and allow their children time to adjust at their own pace. If a child shows signs of emotional distress, such as withdrawal, anxiety, or changes in behavior, it may be helpful to seek professional guidance. Therapists or family counselors can provide valuable support and offer strategies to help the child healthily navigate these emotions. Addressing emotional distress early can prevent long-term issues and help the child feel more comfortable in the evolving family structure. Supporting children through emotional transitions requires empathy, patience, and attentiveness. Encourage them to express their emotions and validate their feelings, even if they are negative. Let them know it's okay to feel angry, sad, or confused, and give them the space to process their emotions without fear of judgment. Providing reassurance that they are loved and their feelings matter helps them build resilience and adaptability.

Introducing a new partner requires sensitivity, patience, and a deep understanding of the child's emotional needs. Prioritizing stability, maintaining open communication, and ensuring that the child feels valued, single parents can help mitigate the negative impacts and create an environment where both the child and the new partner can build positive, respectful relationships.

Acknowledging and addressing the complexities of family transitions allows children to feel supported and understood. With the right strategies, parents can successfully navigate the challenges of integrating a new partner into the family while preserving their child's emotional well-being and fostering a healthy, cohesive family dynamic.

Chapter 9

Interaction Between the Partner and Child

When a new partner enters the home, safeguarding the child's emotional and physical well-being is paramount. Establishing clear boundaries ensures trust and security, while inappropriate interactions if left unchecked, can have lasting adverse effects. Below are strategies for prevention and the importance of supporting the child throughout this transition.

Prevention Strategies

From the start, it is critical to establish clear expectations regarding the partner's role in the child's life. This includes defining the partner's limits, such as avoiding disciplinary responsibilities and refraining from overly personal interactions without explicit consent from the parent. These boundaries help prevent confusion for the child and clarify what is acceptable to the partner. Boundaries must also cover physical interactions, such as affection and personal space, aligning with what makes the child feel safe and comfortable.

Setting clear boundaries early on establishes a foundation of trust and understanding. Both the partner and the child must know that these boundaries are non-negotiable and serve to protect the child's emotional and physical well-being. Parents should communicate these limits explicitly and ensure the partner and child understand their importance. Parents can create a safe environment for the child to feel comfortable adjusting to the new family dynamic.

Supervision

: Initially, limit your partner's time alone with your child. This not only gives the child time to adjust but also allows trust to build naturally over time. Supervision ensures that all interactions between the child and the new partner remain respectful and appropriate while allowing the parent to observe how their child responds to the partner's presence. Gradually increasing the partner's involvement can help the child develop a sense of security.

Parents should be mindful of the child's comfort level during interactions. By observing how their child behaves when the partner is present—such as body language, facial expressions, and verbal cues— parents can gain valuable insights into how well the child adapts to the new situation. If the child shows signs of discomfort or distress, taking those cues seriously and adjusting the approach accordingly is essential. The goal is to create a gradual, respectful relationship-building process, ensuring that the child's emotional needs are prioritized.

Communicate Expectations

: It is essential to have open conversations with your partner about boundaries and expectations. Explain clearly what is acceptable regarding their interactions with your child. This will prevent misunderstandings and ensure that everyone is on the same page. Expectations should be revisited regularly to ensure the partner and child are comfortable with the evolving relationship. Clear communication is the key to preventing potential conflicts or missteps. Set aside time to discuss these expectations with your partner, being as specific as possible about behaviors and actions that are appropriate and those that are not. This dialogue should be ongoing as relationships and circumstances evolve. Encourage your partner to express their thoughts or concerns, and be willing to make adjustments when necessary. Keeping an open line of communication reassures both the partner and child that everyone's comfort and well-being are prioritized.

Listen to Your Child

Children should feel safe expressing concerns or discomfort about a new partner. Open communication encourages children to voice their feelings before minor issues escalate into more significant problems. Be proactive in asking how they feel about the new partner, and take their input seriously, mainly if they express discomfort. Active listening validates their feelings and assures them that their emotional well-being is your priority.

Parents should proactively initiate conversations about the child's feelings regarding the new partner. Instead of waiting for issues to arise, parents should regularly check in with the child and ask open-ended questions about their experiences and emotions. It is crucial for the child's emotional safety to create an environment where the child knows they can speak freely without fear of dismissal or retaliation. Responding with empathy and understanding—rather than immediately trying to solve the problem—will help the child feel heard and valued, which is vital for maintaining trust.

Why It's Important to Hear Both Sides
When concerns about inappropriate interactions arise, listening to the child and the partner is essential. Children may struggle to express themselves wholly or might misinterpret specific actions, while the partner might not be aware of crossing boundaries. By listening to both sides, parents can make well-informed decisions, address misunderstandings, and prevent damaging consequences to the family dynamic. Hearing both sides ensures that parents can address concerns objectively. Children may feel threatened by a new dynamic or misinterpret certain gestures, and partners may unintentionally cross lines due to a lack of understanding of the child's comfort

levels. By listening attentively to the child's and the partner's perspectives, parents can navigate misunderstandings more effectively, allowing them to mediate and make adjustments reflecting the child's best interest. The goal is to create a balanced environment where all voices are heard, but the child's safety remains the top priority.

Support Emotionally

It is crucial to help the child throughout this process. Even if subtle signs of distress appear, such as changes in behavior, withdrawal, or reluctance to be around the partner, parents should take these cues seriously. Validating the child's feelings by addressing the issue head-on fosters trust and ensures the child feels protected. Letting the child know that their well-being comes first can help them navigate the emotions they're experiencing as new dynamics develop. Pay close attention to changes in your child's behavior that may signal discomfort. Behavioral shifts such as becoming withdrawn, exhibiting increased anxiety, or avoiding interactions with the new partner can be signs that the child is struggling with the transition. It is crucial to address these issues proactively by having open, empathetic conversations and making necessary adjustments. Reassure the child that their feelings are valid and they have the right to feel safe in their home. This support builds trust for a healthy relationship between the child, the parent, and the new partner.

The Long-Term Impact of Inappropriate Interactions

If inappropriate interactions are left unaddressed, they can cause long-term emotional and psychological damage. Children may lose their sense of safety, which can lead to anxiety, mistrust, or difficulty forming healthy relationships later in life. Remaining vigilant and responsive to a child's emotional cues helps mitigate these risks. It reinforces the parent-child bond, laying a foundation of trust and emotional security that will benefit the child well into adulthood.

Inappropriate interactions, even minor ones, can affect a child's emotional well-being. Children who grow up in environments where they feel unsafe or unheard are more likely to develop issues with trust, anxiety, and self-worth. Parents can prevent these adverse outcomes by addressing inappropriate behaviors immediately and ensuring that the child's emotional needs are prioritized. Establishing a home environment where respect, empathy, and boundaries are consistently upheld creates a secure space for the child to grow into a confident, emotionally healthy adult.

Conclusion

Preventing inappropriate interactions between a new partner and a child is about setting boundaries and creating a safe, open environment where children feel heard and valued. By being attentive to the child's needs, establishing clear roles for the partner, and intervening when necessary, parents can ensure that their children maintain their emotional security and well-being during this adjustment period.

Building a healthy family dynamic requires patience, open communication, and a commitment to the child's well-being. Parents must be willing to establish boundaries, listen actively, and address concerns promptly. By doing so, they can create an environment where children feel safe and supported, even in the face of significant changes. The child's emotional health should always be at the forefront, ensuring they grow up feeling valued, protected, and empowered to navigate their relationships confidently.

Chapter 10

New Partner, Their Children, Your Child

When introducing a new partner into the household, safeguarding your child's emotional and physical well-being is paramount. However, it's equally important to consider interactions between your child and the partner's children, especially older ones. Inappropriate behavior can stem not only from the partner but also from the partner's children, potentially leading to harmful dynamics.

Recognizing the Potential for Inappropriate Behavior from Older Children

Older children of the partner may intentionally engage in inappropriate behaviors toward younger children or because of a lack of boundaries. The dynamics of blended families can be complicated, especially when children from different households are expected to share space and establish new relationships. Emotional tension, rivalry, or power struggles can create a fertile ground for inappropriate interactions.

For instance, an older child may attempt to assert dominance over younger children, bullying them or making them uncomfortable. In other cases, older children might model inappropriate behaviors they've observed or feel emboldened to cross personal boundaries because they perceive less strict supervision. These actions can include emotional manipulation, physical intimidation, or more serious breaches of personal space and safety.

Setting Boundaries and Clear Expectations for All Children

To prevent these situations, it's crucial to establish clear boundaries and rules for all children in the household—whether biological, stepchildren, or children from the partner's previous relationships. These boundaries should include:

Personal Space and Privacy There must be clear spoken and, if necessary, written expectations about respecting each other's personal space, belongings, and rooms. All children should understand that they must knock before entering each other's spaces and respect privacy.

Appropriate Behavior: Define what constitutes respectful and proper behavior between children. This includes speaking to one another, interacting physically, and resolving conflicts.

Respect for Authority Ensure that all children understand and respect the parental figures in the household, but also make it clear that no child should attempt to discipline or control another. Creating an environment of mutual respect is crucial to maintaining a healthy household dynamic.

Supervision and Monitoring of Interactions

Supervision is vital in the early stages of blending families. Parents should be attentive to how the children interact and step in quickly if inappropriate behavior is observed. Monitoring these early interactions helps identify problematic behaviors before they escalate into more severe issues. Encourage open communication between the children and the adults in the household so they feel safe reporting anything that makes them uncomfortable.

While direct supervision isn't always possible, establishing times when the family spends time together can provide natural opportunities for adults to observe the dynamics. Pay attention to any shifts in behavior—such as withdrawal, reluctance to interact, or mood changes—that may indicate a child feels unsafe or uncomfortable.

Creating Safe Spaces for Communication

It's essential to create an environment where children can express their concerns without fear of repercussions. Children, especially younger ones, may hesitate to speak up if they feel intimidated by older children or worry they won't be believed. As a parent, please encourage your child to come to you with any problems or concerns and take their feelings seriously. Regularly check in with your child to ask how they feel about the family dynamic. Simple, open-ended questions like, "How are you feeling about things at home?" or "Is there anything bothering you?" can create a pathway for honest dialogue.

Intervening and Addressing Problems
If you notice inappropriate behavior from an older child, it's important to intervene immediately. Address the issue calmly and firmly, ensuring the child understands why their actions are unacceptable. This intervention must come from both you and your partner, showing a united front and reinforcing that inappropriate behavior will not be tolerated. In more severe cases, such as physical or emotional bullying, professional counseling or mediation may be necessary. Blended families often benefit from family therapy, where all members can work on communication, boundary-setting, and conflict resolution.

Conclusion: Prioritizing Emotional and Physical Safety in Blended Families The process of blending families can be complex, and the emotional safety of all children in the household should be a top priority. Parents can prevent inappropriate behavior from their partner or children by setting clear boundaries, supervising interactions, and fostering open communication. Maintaining vigilance and offering consistent emotional support ensures that all children feel safe, respected, and valued in the new family structure.

Chapter 11

The Way To Move Forward

The frequent introduction of new partners into a child's life has profound emotional and psychological effects, often leading to feelings of instability, confusion, and insecurity. For single parents, dating and forming new relationships is a natural process, but these transitions must be handled carefully to protect the well-being of their children.

Adopting a child-centered approach is one of the first steps toward minimizing negative impacts. Children thrive on stability and routine, and disruptions to these foundational elements can be deeply unsettling. Therefore, parents should be intentional about how and when they introduce a new partner to their children. A thoughtful approach—one where a partner is introduced only after a serious commitment has been established—allows children to feel more secure and reduces the likelihood of emotional upheaval.

Open communication is another cornerstone of protecting children during these transitions. When a new partner enters their parent's life, children often experience confusion, insecurity, or jealousy. Regular, age-appropriate conversations with children about these changes can help them process their emotions and feel included in the evolving family dynamics. Ensuring the child understands that their relationship with their parent remains a priority fosters a sense of safety and prevents feelings of abandonment or neglect. It is also essential to maintain consistency in routines and discipline. A household where rules, discipline, and daily routines fluctuate based on the presence of a new partner can lead to frustration, confusion, and behavioral issues in children. Children need a consistent environment to feel grounded, especially during emotionally vulnerable periods. Consistent bedtime routines, family rituals, and discipline strategies offer them a sense of normalcy, even when other aspects of life are changing.

For single parents who feel unsure how to introduce a new partner, seeking professional guidance can be valuable. Family counselors, child psychologists, or support groups can offer strategies for navigating these complex dynamics, ensuring the child and the parent have the tools to maintain emotional well-being. Professional help can be especially critical if children exhibit signs of distress, such as anxiety, withdrawal, or behavioral issues, as it can provide them with a safe space to express their feelings and develop healthy coping mechanisms.

Another critical factor to consider is the role of the new partner. Clear boundaries should be set regarding their involvement in the child's life, especially in areas like discipline. A new partner should not take on parental responsibilities too quickly, as this can disrupt the parent-child dynamic and create feelings of resentment. Building trust and rapport with the child should gradually be rooted in mutual respect and understanding. It is also essential to recognize that every family is unique. How children respond to new partners will vary based on age, temperament, past experiences, and the strength of the parent-child bond. Single parents must remain attuned to their child's emotional state throughout the process and be prepared to adjust their approach based on their child's needs.

While the road ahead may present challenges, single parents can shape their children's emotional health by being thoughtful and deliberate in their actions. Parents can help their children build the secure, trusting relationships they need to thrive despite the complexities of modern family dynamics by focusing on stability, communication, and consistency.

Finally, single parents should remember they are not alone in navigating these situations. Whether through professional support, peer groups, or family networks, resources are available to help parents and children work through the emotional and practical challenges of blended family life. The journey may require patience and adaptability. However, with careful planning and a deep commitment to their child's well-being, parents can foster an environment of love, trust, and security—providing a solid foundation for their child's future relationships and emotional resilience.

Chapter 12

Building Healthy Family Dynamics

Building healthy family dynamics requires consistent effort, open communication, and long-term strategies that can adapt to changing needs over time. Families are unique, and what works for one might not work for another. However, there are common approaches that can help cultivate a nurturing environment for all members, enabling them to thrive individually and as a cohesive unit.

1. Prioritize Quality Time Together

Spending quality time as a family strengthens bonds and creates a sense of belonging. Activities like family meals, game nights, weekend outings, or simply having discussions without distractions can foster a sense of unity. Making family time a non-negotiable priority demonstrates that each member is valued and creates opportunities for positive interactions and deeper connections. Quality time can be simple and inexpensive. Simple activities like cooking together, gardening, or walking in the neighborhood can be as meaningful. The key is to be fully present— putting away phones, turning off the

TV, and focusing on each other. Families can build strong memories that last a lifetime, creating consistent routines for spending time together.

2. Practice Open and Honest Communication

Effective communication is the cornerstone of healthy relationships. Encourage every family member to express their feelings, thoughts, and concerns without fear of judgment or retribution. Active listening is vital— when one person speaks, others should listen attentively, showing empathy and respect. Setting aside regular times to discuss issues openly and celebrate successes as a family builds trust and understanding.

To foster open communication, create a safe space where everyone feels heard. This can be as simple as a weekly family meeting or a daily check-in. Encourage children to articulate their emotions by using "I feel" statements, which helps them communicate effectively without placing blame. By validating each other's experiences and feelings, families can strengthen their emotional bonds and promote a culture of openness.

3. Set Clear Boundaries and Roles

Healthy boundaries and defined roles provide structure and security. Each member should understand their responsibilities within the family while knowing their personal space and autonomy are respected. Establishing boundaries helps prevent misunderstandings and conflicts, while clearly defined roles ensure everyone contributes meaningfully through chores, emotional support, or shared decision-making.

Boundaries should be flexible enough to adapt to changing needs. For example, as children grow older, their roles and responsibilities may shift, requiring parents to adjust expectations accordingly. Open discussions about boundaries help ensure everyone is comfortable and understands their role in maintaining a harmonious household. Respecting each other's privacy and individuality is also key to fostering a supportive environment.

4. Embrace Conflict Resolution
Conflicts are natural in any relationship, and families are no exception. Embracing healthy conflict resolution means approaching disagreements with a problem-solving mindset instead of avoiding or escalating them. Teach children to express their disagreements respectfully and model how to negotiate and find common ground. Learning to resolve conflicts constructively strengthens family bonds and reduces resentment.

When conflicts arise, it is essential to stay calm and focus on the issue rather than the person. Use "I" statements to express feelings without blaming others, and encourage family members to listen actively to one another's perspectives. Families can also benefit from establishing ground rules for resolving conflicts, such as taking turns speaking and avoiding interrupting. Families can grow stronger and more resilient by working together to find mutually acceptable solutions.

5. Foster Emotional Intelligence and Empathy

Encouraging emotional intelligence—the ability to identify, understand, and manage emotions—is vital for building healthy family dynamics. Parents and caregivers should model empathy, helping children understand and validate their and others' feelings. Family members who practice empathy can better support each other, fostering a more caring and nurturing environment.

To cultivate emotional intelligence, teach children to recognize and name their emotions. Please encourage them to think about how others might feel in different situations, which can help them develop empathy. Modeling empathy as a parent—by acknowledging and validating your child's emotions—sets a powerful example. Emotional intelligence helps family relationships and equips children with skills to navigate social situations outside the home.

6. Encourage Individual Growth and Autonomy

While family unity is essential, it is equally vital to recognize and support each member's individuality. Encourage hobbies, passions, and personal goals, and celebrate achievements, big or small. Allowing space for individual growth helps each family member develop a strong sense of self, ultimately contributing to a healthier family dynamic.

Supporting individual growth means recognizing that each family member has unique strengths, interests, and aspirations. Parents can encourage autonomy by allowing children to make age-appropriate decisions and take on new challenges. This helps children build confidence and independence. Celebrating each member's successes—whether a school achievement, a work promotion, or a personal milestone—reinforces the importance of personal growth within the family context.

7. Create Family Rituals and Traditions
Rituals and traditions help create lasting memories and give families something to look forward to, which can strengthen connections. Whether it's celebrating birthdays in a particular way, seasonal traditions, or small daily rituals like bedtime stories, these moments build a shared family identity that brings comfort and joy.

Family rituals don't have to be elaborate—consistency and meaning matter. For example, having a special dinner every Friday night or an annual family trip can create cherished memories. Traditions provide a sense of continuity, especially during change or stress. They also remind the family of its values and the importance of spending time together, reinforcing the bonds that hold the family together.

8. Model Healthy Relationships

Children learn about relationships by observing the adults around them. Demonstrating respect, love, and support in your relationships—whether with a partner, friends, or extended family—sets a powerful example. Treat others with kindness, communicate effectively, and demonstrate problem-solving skills to help children understand healthy relationships.

Modeling healthy relationships also involves showing how to manage disagreements constructively. Let children see that conflict is a normal part of relationships and can be resolved through respectful dialogue. Show affection and appreciation for your partner or other family members, and make an effort to involve children in activities that promote positive interactions. Children learn how to build and maintain positive connections by witnessing healthy relationships.

9. Foster a Culture of Gratitude and Positivity

. Cultivating a culture of gratitude within the family can have a significant positive impact. Encourage family members to share things they are grateful for regularly. Emphasizing positivity and celebrating small victories can help family members stay resilient through difficult times, providing a sense of optimism and security.

One way to foster gratitude is to create a family gratitude ritual, such as sharing one thing you're thankful for during dinner or before bedtime. Practicing gratitude helps shift the focus away from problems and toward the positive aspects of life. Celebrating achievements—no matter how small—reinforces a positive mindset and helps family members feel appreciated. This positivity can be a powerful tool for coping with challenges and maintaining a supportive family environment.

10. Seek Support When Needed
. Recognizing when to seek outside help is essential to maintaining healthy family dynamics. Whether it's family counseling, support groups, or educational resources, seeking professional guidance shows strength, not weakness. It demonstrates a commitment to growth and well-being, which can positively influence the entire family.

There is no shame in asking for help when challenges feel overwhelming. Family counseling can provide a neutral space for members to express their feelings and work through issues with the guidance of a trained professional. Support groups can also offer valuable insights and a sense of community for families facing similar challenges. By being proactive about seeking support, families can address issues before they escalate and continue to grow together in a healthy, positive way.

Building healthy family dynamics is a lifelong journey that requires flexibility, patience, and consistent effort. Nurturing communication, understanding, and respect can help families create a supportive environment where every member feels valued and loved.

Chapter 13

Rebuilding: The Blended Family

Blending two families can be a beautiful opportunity to create a loving, supportive environment. However, the process of merging families is rarely without its challenges. When two different households, each with its traditions, dynamics, and history, come together, the journey can be fraught with difficulties that can impact every family member. Successfully rebuilding a family unit as a blended family requires patience, understanding, and a willingness to navigate the inevitable emotional complexities.

Navigating the Complexity of Different Parenting Styles

One of the most common pitfalls of blending families is the clash of different parenting styles. Each parent may come into the relationship with their beliefs about discipline, boundaries, and child-rearing, which can lead to conflicts between the parents and the children involved. Children receiving mixed messages about rules and expectations can create confusion and frustration, leading to resistance or behavioral issues.

For example, one parent may believe in strict discipline and clear consequences, while the other prefers a more lenient approach that encourages open communication and negotiation. This disparity can make it challenging for children to know what is expected of them and who to listen to, undermining the sense of stability that is very important during the transition to a blended family. Parents must have open conversations about their parenting styles before blending with their families to avoid this pitfall. Finding common ground or creating shared family rules that respect both parents' values is vital. Consistency is crucial for children to feel secure in their environment, so even if parents have differing approaches, it's essential to agree on fundamental principles and present a united front. This process of compromise and cooperation can also serve as a powerful example for the children to navigate differences within a relationship.

The Challenge of Forming Bonds and Establishing Trust

Another major pitfall in rebuilding a family unit as a blended family is the challenge of forming bonds between step-siblings and between children and their new step-parents. Building these relationships takes time, and expecting immediate closeness can lead to disappointment and resentment. Children may feel loyalty to their biological parents and may be resistant to accepting a step-parent's authority or affection. This resistance can manifest in withdrawal, defiance, or overt hostility toward the new family members.

Blended family siblings may also struggle to connect, especially if they have different interests or feel forced into relationships they aren't ready for. Sibling rivalry can become more pronounced in a blended family, mainly if children think their parents' attention is now divided. This rivalry can lead to tension and conflict, making the home environment stressful for everyone involved. Patience is critical to successfully building bonds within a blended family. Parents must understand that relationships take time and cannot be forced. Encouraging shared activities, such as family outings or game nights, can create natural interactions and bonding opportunities without putting too much pressure on the children. It's also essential for parents to have one-on-one time with their biological children to reassure them of their unique and irreplaceable place in their lives.

Managing Expectations and Avoiding Unrealistic Assumptions

Blending a family often comes with certain expectations and hopes—perhaps everyone will immediately get along, that children will be excited about the changes, or that the new family will quickly feel like a cohesive unit. These expectations, while understandable, can set everyone up for disappointment if they aren't realistic. It's natural for children to need time to adjust, and there may be resistance or reluctance as they navigate new relationships and changes to their routines.

Parents should avoid making assumptions about how quickly their children or their new partner's children will adapt to the new family structure. Some children may take longer to warm up to their step-parent or step-siblings, while others may seem to adjust quickly but experience emotional challenges later.

It's important to remember that every child's processes change differently, and their feelings should be respected, even if they seem harmful or inconvenient to their parent's new relationship.

Managing expectations also means understanding that setbacks are normal. As everyone learns how to coexist, there may be moments of conflict, hurt feelings, and challenges. Instead of seeing these moments as failures, parents should view them as opportunities for growth and learning. Keeping communication open, validating each family member's feelings, and showing empathy can help the family constructively work through these challenges.

Addressing the Fear of Replacement and Loyalty Conflicts

Children in blended families may struggle with

loyalty conflict, fearing that accepting a step-parent or forming a bond with step-siblings means betraying their biological parent. This fear can be incredibly intense if the other biological parent is still actively involved in their life. Children may worry that showing affection toward a step-parent will hurt their other parent's feelings or that they are disloyal by enjoying the new family structure.

These loyalty conflicts can create emotional barriers that prevent children from fully accepting the blended family. They may act out in unreasonable or overly defensive ways, but these behaviors often reflect their internal struggle to navigate these conflicting emotions. Parents need to acknowledge these feelings rather than dismiss them. Openly discussing these fears and reassuring children that they are not expected to replace anyone can help ease their anxiety.

Stepparents should also avoid trying to replace the biological parent. Instead, they can focus on building a unique, supportive relationship that complements the child's family ties. Blended families can foster stronger connections over time by creating a safe space where children feel their emotions are validated and their loyalties are respected.

Dealing with Grief and Unresolved Emotions
Blending a family often requires children to deal with grief or unresolved emotions related to their previous

family structure. Whether the family was disrupted by divorce, separation, or the loss of a parent, these emotions can significantly impact how a child reacts to a new family dynamic. If children feel that their grief is being overlooked or that their feelings are not being acknowledged, they may resist accepting the blended family. Parents and step-parents must recognize that children may need time to process their feelings about the changes. Providing opportunities for them to talk about their emotions—without judgment or pressure to feel a certain way—can help them healthily work through their grief. Family therapy can also be beneficial, offering a supportive environment where children can explore their feelings and learn how to adjust to the changes in their family.

Parents should also know that grief may resurface during significant family events like holidays, birthdays, or other milestones. These moments can bring up memories, causing children to feel renewed loss. Acknowledging and allowing space for these feelings can help children feel heard and supported, even during difficult times.

Creating New Traditions While Respecting the Old

One way to blend a family's holidays successfully is to create new family traditions that everyone can enjoy. New traditions can foster a sense of unity and belonging, allowing each family member to feel part of something special. However, respecting and preserving old traditions that hold meaning for the children is equally important. Abruptly changing or eliminating traditions can make children feel like they are losing another part of their former lives, adding to their sense of loss and resistance.

Blending traditions from both families allows everyone to contribute something unique, creating a new family culture that honors the past while embracing the future. For example, if one family always had a special Sunday breakfast, continuing that tradition while incorporating a new element—such as everyone taking turns choosing the menu—can help maintain a sense of continuity while also building something new together. Balancing the old traditions with the new may help children feel that their history is valued, which can ease their transition into a blended family.

Addressing Blended Sibling Rivalry and Jealousy
Blended families often face the challenge of sibling rivalry and jealousy as children navigate their place within the newly formed family structure. These feelings can arise for various reasons, including competition for parental attention, differences in treatment, and the struggle to adapt to new relationships. Addressing these issues proactively fosters a harmonious blended family environment where each child feels valued and secure.

Understanding the Root Causes of Rivalry and Jealousy

Sibling rivalry and jealousy in blended families often stem from the fear of being replaced or losing the exclusive bond they once had with their biological parent. When new step-siblings enter the picture, children may feel threatened, believing they must compete for their parent's time, attention, and affection. These emotions can lead to tension and conflict as children attempt to assert their position within the family.

Differences in parenting styles or household rules can also contribute to rivalry and jealousy. When children from different backgrounds are suddenly expected to live together under one roof, disparities in expectations can lead to resentment. One child may perceive their step-sibling being treated more favorably, even if this perception is inaccurate. Parents must understand these underlying fears and address them with empathy and patience.

Case Study 4: Anna, Age 16

Anna's father remarried when she was 14, introducing a stepmother and her teenage children into their home. While Anna initially hoped to gain new siblings and create a more prominent, supportive family, the reality was far different from her expectations. The transition brought significant emotional challenges, leaving Anna feeling like an outsider in her home. Her new step-siblings often formed their alliances, excluding Anna from activities and making her feel isolated. This sense of exclusion and the sudden changes in her family dynamic left Anna struggling to find her place.

Anna's father, preoccupied with his new marriage and trying to make everyone feel comfortable, was unaware of how deeply Anna was struggling. He divided his attention between his new wife, her children, and Anna, unintentionally leaving Anna feeling neglected. She felt that her father focused more on making his new family work than understanding her needs. The lack of direct communication only deepened Anna's feelings of loneliness and resentment, creating an emotional distance between her and her father.

In response to these emotions, Anna began acting out. She argued frequently with her father, feeling unheard and misunderstood. The arguments often revolved around her step-siblings or her father's perceived favoritism, which only added to the tension in the household. To escape the uncomfortable environment at home, Anna started skipping school and distancing herself from her friends.

Her grades began to suffer, and her once bright and outgoing personality dulled under the weight of her emotional turmoil. Anna felt like she was losing her relationship with her father —the one she had always depended on. She feared that she was being replaced and that her father's love for her had diminished in favor of his new family. This fear of abandonment and her sense of not belonging led Anna to withdraw emotionally, refusing to engage in family activities and isolating herself in her room. The household, meant to be a place of comfort and security, had become a source of stress and sadness for Anna.

Seeing Anna's emotional decline and recognizing the growing tension within the family, Anna's stepmother suggested they attend family therapy. Although initially resistant, Anna eventually agreed to participate. The therapy sessions provided a safe, neutral space for Anna to express her feelings. For the first time, Anna could voice her frustrations about feeling left out, her fears of losing her father's affection, and her sense of being a stranger in her home. Her father, in turn, listened without interruption, and it became clear to him how much Anna had been struggling.

Family therapy also allowed Anna's father to reflect on his actions. He realized that, in his effort to create harmony with his new family, he had inadvertently neglected Anna's needs and failed to recognize the emotional challenges she was facing. With the therapist's guidance, he learned how to be more present for Anna, setting aside dedicated time just for the two of them. They began to reestablish their bond through weekly outings, which allowed them to reconnect without the pressures of the blended family dynamic.

The family sessions also involved Anna's stepmother and step-siblings, allowing everyone to share their feelings and understand each other's perspectives. Anna's stepmother tried to reach out to her, acknowledging that the transition had been difficult and expressing her desire to build a positive relationship. The step-siblings, who hadn't fully realized their exclusion's impact on Anna, began to include her more in their activities, trying to bridge the gap between them.

Slowly, Anna began to adapt to the changes. She felt more understood and valued by her father, stepmother, and step-siblings. The therapy sessions helped the family establish new routines and traditions that included everyone, giving Anna a renewed sense of belonging. Her relationship with her father improved significantly, as he consciously prioritized her needs to ensure she never felt left out again.

Anna also learned coping strategies to manage her emotions for positive expressions and interactions. The therapist introduced her to journaling to express her feelings, which helped her process her emotions constructively. She also learned how to communicate her needs without arguments, making her interactions with her father and stepmother more positive. As Anna began to feel more secure in her place within the family, her behavior at school improved, and she started reconnecting with her friends.

This case study highlights the emotional complexities that can arise when blending families, particularly for teenagers who may already be navigating the challenges of adolescence. Anna's experience underscores the importance of open communication, empathy, and intentionally including every family member during such transitions. By listening to and adjusting to Anna's needs, her father and stepmother created a more inclusive and supportive environment, allowing her to feel secure and valued again.

Families in similar situations can learn from Anna's story. The key to successfully blending families is acknowledging the difficulties involved and giving each member the time and space to adjust. Open communication, family therapy, and ensuring no one feels overlooked are essential to building a cohesive, loving, blended family. Parents need to remember that each child's emotional needs are unique, and addressing those needs with empathy and understanding can make all the difference in fostering a positive and supportive family environment.

Strategies to Mitigate Rivalry and Jealousy

1. Open Communication and Active Listening

Encouraging open communication is vital to addressing sibling rivalry and jealousy. Children need to feel that their voices are heard and that their feelings are valid. Parents should create opportunities for one-on-one conversations where children can express their concerns without fear of judgment. By listening actively, parents can better understand what drives their child's jealousy or frustration, allowing them to address the root causes effectively.

Family meetings can also be an effective way to encourage communication among siblings. These meetings provide a structured environment where each family member can express their thoughts and feelings, allowing them to work through issues together. This helps children feel they are part of the solution and that their opinions matter.

2. Establishing Fair and Consistent Rules

One significant trigger of sibling rivalry is perceived favoritism. To mitigate this, parents should establish household rules that apply consistently to all children, regardless of their biological background. Consistent rules and expectations help create a sense of fairness, reducing the likelihood of resentment between siblings. It's also essential to involve the children in making some of these rules, which encourages a sense of ownership and responsibility.

If children feel that the rules are fair and that everyone is being held to the same standards, they are less likely to harbor feelings of jealousy. Consistency also helps establish stability, particularly in blended families where children may already adjust to significant changes.

3. Encourage Individuality and One-on-One Time

Blended families must balance fostering family unity and recognizing each child's individuality. Encouraging children to pursue their interests and celebrating their unique talents can help reduce feelings of rivalry. Each child should have opportunities to express themselves and engage in activities that make them feel unique and valued.

Additionally, spending dedicated one-on-one time with each child is crucial for maintaining strong parent-child bonds. When children feel that they are getting individual attention from their parents, they are less likely to feel threatened by the presence of a step-sibling. Whether it's a weekly outing, a particular bedtime routine, or simply setting aside time to talk, these moments can reassure children that their relationship with their parents is still essential and unique.

4. Foster Teamwork and Cooperation

Encouraging siblings to work together as a team can help reduce rivalry and build positive relationships. Parents can foster cooperation by creating opportunities for siblings to collaborate on tasks, such as cooking a meal, working on a family project, or playing cooperative games. These shared experiences can help children see each other as allies rather than competitors.

Parents should also recognize and celebrate instances of positive sibling interactions. Praising children when they help each other or show kindness can reinforce these behaviors and encourage them to continue. Over time, these positive experiences can help build a sense of camaraderie and strengthen sibling bonds.

5. Acknowledge and Validate Emotions

Parents should acknowledge the complex emotions that children may feel when adjusting to a blended family. Jealousy, fear, and even anger are normal reactions to significant changes, and children need to know that it's okay to feel this way. Validating these emotions—rather than dismissing them—can help children feel understood and supported.

Parents can help children process these emotions by talking through their feelings and providing reassurance. For example, suppose a child feels jealous because they believe their step-sibling is receiving more attention. In that case, the parent can acknowledge this feeling and explain the situation to reassure the child of their importance in the family. Emotional validation helps children feel more secure and reduces the likelihood of acting out due to unresolved feelings.

6. Create New Family Traditions

Creating new family traditions can help blended families build a sense of unity and belonging. Whether it's a weekly movie night, a special holiday ritual, or a family outing, these shared experiences help foster a sense of togetherness. When children feel part of creating these new traditions, they can feel more connected to the blended family.

Respecting and incorporating old traditions from each family is also essential, as this helps children maintain a sense of continuity and identity. Blending old and new traditions allows children to feel their history is honored while embracing the new family structure.

Building Harmony in Blended Families

Sibling rivalry and jealousy are common challenges in blended families, but parents can constructively address these issues with intentionality and empathy. By fostering open communication, establishing fair rules, encouraging individuality, and creating opportunities for positive interactions, parents can help their children navigate the complexities of blended families.

Building a successful blended family requires patience and a commitment to understanding each child's unique needs. By providing a supportive and consistent environment, parents can help their children develop strong, positive relationships with their step-siblings, creating a harmonious and loving family unit where everyone feels valued and secure.

Rebuilding a family unit as a blended family comes with many potential pitfalls, but with empathy, patience, and clear communication, these challenges can be navigated successfully. Understanding that each family member processes change differently, respecting existing relationships, and gradually building new bonds are essential to creating a cohesive and loving family environment.

By setting realistic expectations, validating emotions, and being willing to work through difficult moments, parents and step-parents can create a blended family where each member feels valued, heard, and secure.

While the journey may be complex, the reward of creating a supportive, unified family is worth the effort. It provides a foundation of love and stability that will benefit every family member for years.

In Summary

Raising children as a single parent or within a blended family comes with unique challenges. Still, with intentionality and empathy, creating a healthy, supportive environment that fosters balanced, successful children is possible. Whether a single parent chooses to remain single or remarry, the focus must be on providing stability, open communication, and unwavering emotional support to help children thrive. The foundation of a successful family unit starts with prioritizing the child's emotional needs. Single parents must ensure their children feel heard, valued, and loved unconditionally. This means building strong, trusting relationships where children feel secure expressing their emotions, fears, and needs. For single parents considering new relationships, it is crucial to be mindful of how these changes impact their children, ensuring that new partners are introduced gradually and thoughtfully only after a serious commitment.

Creating a consistent environment is vital in helping children feel secure. Consistency in routines, discipline, and family traditions helps foster a sense of predictability that is especially important in times of change. Single parents should maintain familiar routines, such as regular mealtimes, bedtime rituals, and quality one-on-one time with each child. These moments of stability reinforce a child's sense of belonging and provide reassurance that, despite changes in the family structure, they remain a top priority.

Open communication is another cornerstone of a successful family unit. Parents should create an environment where children feel comfortable respectfully discussing their thoughts and concerns without fear of judgment. In blended families, open communication is crucial, as children may experience conflicting emotions, such as loyalty conflicts or jealousy. By encouraging honest conversations and validating each child's feelings, parents can help them navigate these emotions healthily.

Parents must also recognize the importance of building trust over time. Whether introducing a new partner or helping children adjust to new step-siblings, forming bonds within a blended family requires patience. New relationships cannot be rushed; they should be nurtured through shared experiences and consistent efforts to understand each family member's unique needs. Step-parents should focus on building a supportive relationship based on empathy and respect rather than attempting to replace a biological parent.

Ultimately, a successful family unit—single or blended—relies on empathy, intentionality, and the willingness to adapt to the evolving needs of each child. Single parents can create an environment where their children feel secure, valued, and capable of thriving by prioritizing emotional well-being, maintaining consistency, fostering open communication, and building trust. The journey may be challenging, but the reward of raising confident, balanced, and resilient children is well worth the effort, providing a solid foundation for them to build fulfilling lives of their own.

I leave you with the most important message:

"Love your children unconditionally."

They reflect you, brought into this world without their choice or opinion. They deserve your unwavering love and support every step of the way. Teach them to respect you, others, and, most importantly, themselves.

ABOUT THE AUTHOR

'Whose Shoes Are These?' explores the complex emotional journey of children raised by single parents who often introduce new partners into their lives. Through powerful insights, this book emphasizes the importance of recognizing and addressing the challenges faced by single and blended families early on to nurture emotional growth and stability in children.

Hailing from Canton, Ohio, Holly's passion for this writing centers on possible childhood traumas and how addressing their effects can be mitigated through early awareness and intervention.

www.ingramcontent.com/pod-product-compliance
Lightning Source LLC
Chambersburg PA
CBHW031420150726
47989CB00002B/734